# The Secret Verse

## The Wealth That Lasts

*Eugene Ogaga-Oghene*

WESTBOW®
PRESS
A DIVISION OF THOMAS NELSON
& ZONDERVAN

All scripture quotations are taken from the
New International Version (NIV) of the Holy Bible;
except otherwise stated

WestBow Press books may be ordered through booksellers or by contacting:

WestBow Press
A Division of Thomas Nelson & Zondervan
1663 Liberty Drive
Bloomington, IN 47403
www.westbowpress.com
1 (866) 928-1240

ISBN: 978-1-4908-1577-0 (sc)
ISBN: 978-1-4908-1578-7 (e)

Library of Congress Control Number: 2013921034

Print information available on the last page.

WestBow Press rev. date: 04/15/2015

"DO not store up for yourselves treasures on earth, where moth and rust destroy, and where thieves break in and steal. But store up for yourselves treasures in heaven, where moth and rust do not destroy, and where thieves do not break in and steal.

*Matthew 6:19-20*

*Do not work for food that spoils, but for food that endures to eternal life, which the Son of Man will give you.*

*John 6:27*

*This is God's secret wisdom, a wisdom that has been hidden and that God destined for our glory before time began*

*1 Cor 2:7*

One of the treasures of investment which moth or rust cannot destroy and where thieves cannot break in to steal but stored up in us and for us in heaven; the kind of work that cannot spoil but wells up to everlasting wealth in eternity; the Secret Wisdom of God hidden but destined for us who believe is the investment in ONE-SELF in the true knowledge of the Christ of God, revealed in "The Secret Verse". Author

# Contents

# Dedication

I dedicate this book to Jehovah, the Lord that reveals all things, who made His wisdom simple and clear and to late Pastor Inalegwu and Pastor Sarah Omakwu, President, Family Ministries International and Senior Pastor Family Worship Center, Abuja, Nigeria, the channels through whom this wisdom was exposed in the Discipleship Training School and to all those who desire to change the world through Godly character.

# Acknowledgement

I acknowledge the Almighty God, Jehovah Elo-him, the creator, my maker and sustainer; who has considered me worthy to receive His wisdom for this generation and the next. I acknowledge late Pastor Inalegwu and Pastor Sarah Omakwu who greatly influenced my Christian growth and maturity by nurturing and stabilizing my faith in God.

I am particularly grateful to brother Riel Uben, the instructors and secretariat staff of the Discipleship Training School of the Family Worship Centre, Wuye District, Federal Capital Territory, Abuja, Nigeria, who encouraged me to put my teachings in writing for others to read, learn and grow.

I am particularly grateful to the following Pastor-friends, who toiled day and night to read and re-read the manuscripts and made wonderful suggestions and positive criticisms; Pastor Solomon Yero of the Harvest Field Christian Church International, Abuja, Mrs. Stella Anukam, sister Helen Akula, Sister Hannatu Kayit, sister Elsie Oghenekaro, brother Bidemi, brother Carly Ayuba, of Family Worship Center, Abuja, brother Segun Toluhi, of All Christian Fellowship International, Abuja, and sister Elizabeth Bart-Williams of the Redeemed Christian Church of God, GoodNews Haven, (RCCG),Thamesmed, London England.

Finally, I give thanks to my earthly father Engineer Wilson and my mother Mrs. Julie-Comfort Kokoruwe, my lovely wife Pastor Helen Ogaga-Oghene, and my children, Michael-Aaron, Victor, Soteria, and Monday Mue. They created the atmosphere conducive to write.

# *Foreword*

It is in our hands now, "The Secret Verse". Though the insight Elder Eugene Ogaga-Oghene brings to the reader is called "The Secret Verse", it is actually a revelation of the desired mind and will of God for mankind in today's harassed, confused and deceitful world. This book brings to us the mind of the Holy Spirit in our time. It shows the easy step-by-step essentials to Christian development, which should culminate to maturity in our walk as the adopted sons and daughters of God.

It points the road map to a certain satisfaction, yearnings and cry of the world to see the manifestations of the sons and daughters of God. This empowerment commences from the renewal of our minds, our attitudinal change from the slave, friend, brother mentality to that of maturity and attainment for the manifestation as the sons and daughters of God.

"The Secret Verse" shows the journey and stages of spiritual maturity that we must prepare and attain in order to be able to overcome the evil and corruptions of this idolatrous and rebellious world. It shows the various levels of Christian maturity, the limitations, the extent God can use us, and how to live a Godly prosperous life.

This book challenges us to grow up to manifest the spirit of the children of God, to win the confidence of God for Him to entrust to us what mankind lost in the garden of Eden. True life, which is, Godly consciousness, dominion, power, control to rule the earth, Love, Obedience, Wisdom, Peace will make us act as God's children on earth. This is the treasure found in "The Secret Verse", the character and nature of God that mankind lost for ages that was revealed through His Son Jesus Christ.

I prayerfully recommend this book to everyone who sincerely desires to grow and manifest victoriously here on earth. It is an understandable and easy to read set of principles. As we read, I believe the Holy Spirit will expand our knowledge of God's intention for us and make all grace abound to us for growth.

**Okechukwu Emmanuel,**
**Pastor Growing Pillars Assembly and**
**member Intercessors for Nigeria(IFN), Abuja**

# Introduction

"The Secret Verse" is the first of four in the "Wealth that Lasts" series of books by Mr. Eugene Ogaga-Oghene. The "Wealth that lasts" series of books identifies four areas of genuine treasures of investments that last forever, which thieves cannot Break –in to steal or moth and rust destroy-the investments that last forever!

The investments that last forever are in treasures that are available to everyone, so close, yet neglected; they seem hidden but are open to all who care to seek by reading these books with an unbiased mind.

"The Secret Verse" points to us as the first area of everlasting investment, to ensure we mature into the fullness of God's purpose and plans. It emphasizes that until we grow into full maturity we cannot enjoy the treasures in us. This book outlines how we can invest in ourselves, and the fullness of maturity. Knowledge acquired lasts forever. It directs us to the essentials in life, and how to reduce the energies we expend on painful searches and wrong investments.

"The Secret Verse" tells the awesome story of the slave-servant whom a very wealthy king adopted. By developing the principles revealed in this book, the slave-servant transformed his humble beginnings and became very powerful and highly influential, after inheriting the king who left him the... wealth that lasts forever.

I have been in the midst of believers and watched in earnest when they pray, how they pray and how long it has taken for the prayers to get answered; Some shout and quote the promises of God from His Holy Word, yet get no answers or their prayers take ages to manifest. The prayers of others appear to fall on 'deaf ears' leading to deep frustrations and subsequent decline in their faith.

I began to ponder if all these prayers were not directed to the same God. Many things did not seem clear to me and so I decided to seek God for more insight. It is the results that I have put down in this book.

## "The Secret Verse"

This book reveals deep secrets to quick answers to prayers, and attempts to reduce or possibly put an end to our attitude of fruitless 'shouting' and 'claiming' of the promises of the Word of God. It is a guide in the spiritual journey that the saved man or soul must undertake, through scriptural and Godly principles, to attain maturity. It exposes the fact that the Bible is not merely the Holy Word of God but is also the Book of Godly Principles, which must be mastered before it can be effectively applied to yield positive results. It is about understanding, beliefs, processes, time and maturity. No matter how hard we try only mature trees can bear fruits. Everything in life must go through a process; from beginning to maturity.

The level of maturity and depth of our relationship with God determines how soon the requests we make in prayers are answered. As we read this book may God renew our minds and help us develop Godly relationship with Him so that we can become His son, and daughter in character under His kingdom and authority; which is the ultimate. This is the thrust of "The Secret Verse".

# The Power Of Perception

On this side of heaven, many things can and indeed do happen to us. Our feelings and reactions to such things would normally depend on our perception. Perception will be viewed from the Collins Easy Learning English Study Dictionary as becoming aware or the recognition of something via the senses.

Perception has a great influence on our individual behaviour. Our behaviour is characterized by faith, and our faith has a bearing on or has a direct relationship with our beliefs, and subsequently our character, which makes us. This was adequately explained in "The Victory Within", the series after this. Thus behaviour is the window to perceiving our evident physical and spiritual character which leads to faith and the other characteristics that have been listed in the paragraph below.

These characteristics, namely: feelings, reactions, faith, and belief, exert great impact or influence upon our spirit and our soul on a daily basis. They invariably affect the essence of our existence.

These are inner traits yet they manifest outwardly in such a manner that people around us observe them. Often times, we are described or defined by these traits, and to that extent it could be said that they define who we are or the real man. Consequently, the way and manner we handle these emotional issues can make us live our lives here to the full or diminish the extent to which we enjoy the good things of life.

Our body is a house with various openings through which these traits can either be let in or let out. It is written:

> For **we know** that if our earthly house of this
> tabernacle were dissolved, we have a building of
> God, an house not made with hands, eternal in
> the heavens. 2 Corinthians 5:1 (KJV)

1

And:

> *As you come to him, the living Stone- rejected by men but chosen by God and precious to him- you also, like living stones, are being built into a spiritual house to be a holy priesthood, offering spiritual sacrifices acceptable to God through Jesus Christ.*
>
> *1 Peter 2: 4-5*

The entrances (openings) to the body are the ears, the eyes, the mouth, the nose and our sexual organs including our skin. Through these organs; the bad, the good and the ugly can enter (come in) and go out consciously or unconsciously; because sometimes we might not readily know they have entered or come in until certain situations arise and we begin to exhibit some characteristic behavior. This is the time to contend with them very drastically, if the situations are unpleasant, and entirely undeserved. Attack the issues decisively with an honest resolve and determination to deal squarely with them. It is easier to destroy a thing at its infancy, when it is tender and trying to grow and develop, than when it is mature. As the saying goes, "it is easier to bend or uproot a tree when it is young". (This is also why the enemy attacks dreams at their formative stage; example of Joseph in Gen 37). But where we neglect them, they could grow with deep roots and become very resistant and difficult to take out. Through the lust of the eyes, lust of the flesh and the pride of life some of these issues could enter and manifest.

Bad and ugly traits should be attacked at the initial stage of their manifestation, which starts with our thoughts, evil imaginations and desires. The longer evil thoughts and imaginations and desires are allowed to linger in our minds unchecked, the deeper and stronger the hold they gain over us; eventually propelling us to action.

> *We demolish arguments and every pretension that sets itself up against the knowledge of God, and we take captive every thought to make it obedient to Christ.*
>
> *2 Cor 10:5*

The events that took place after the births of Moses and Jesus Christ aptly illustrate this point. The devil attempted to kill them at infancy. It took the exercise of God's supreme power and purpose to deliver them from the reach and malice of the evil one.

People around us often influence us by the things they do or say. Similarly, our environment influences us particularly by the things we see. It may also be possible that sometimes, we are influenced by what people fail to do and say. Besides the things we see and hear, the things we eat or drink could influence us. We are God's building, a house with many openings. As doors and windows are openings into physical buildings, so also our eyes, ears, mouth, nose and sexual organs are openings to our spiritual house.

When we open them or allow people to open them, certain things will make their way into our minds, which affect our hearts; until we shut them. Prayers alone may not prevent things from entering when they are left open. We must pray and also shut them. Luke 11: 24-26 tells us of the story of the unclean spirit and what happens when we do not shut our gates. Nature abhors a vacuum.

In shutting them we need to fill ourselves with the Word of God and His Holy Spirit. The bigger the living house is, the more openings it may have. Similarly the older we are in the Lord, the more openings may be revealed to us, and we discover many "no- go-areas" in our lives; more openings that should be shut.

Imagine what would have happened if Moses did not "close back" the Red Sea: some Egyptians would have crossed over with them and continued to torment them. This may explain most probably why some born-again Christians still experience torment from the power of darkness: They may have left certain doors still open. (Exodus 14:15-28).

The first contact Adam and Eve had with the forbidden fruit was with their eyes. They *saw* thereby opening the door of the eye for Satan to enter before *hearing* the deceptive suggestions or opinions of the devil, through the door of the ear. It is important to note that there is no particular or fixed format or sequence but could change situationally, however all come to play as the examples below show. Eve heard first, David saw first, Saul fell for pride. Only then did they fall out of God's favour by eating the forbidden fruit, through the door of the mouth.

Similarly, King David *saw* a beautiful, smooth-skinned Bathsheba, and committed adultery, through the door of his sexual organ, thereby sinning against God. The import of these events may be similar to what happened to King Saul, and Judas who betrayed Jesus Christ. Selfish and evil desires; **John 13:27: James 1:14**

Our perception is affected by what we see, what we hear, what we eat or what we do; and it goes through a process of thoughts and imaginations in our mind before it manifests into action. Thus, perception forms the frame for beliefs that manifest or translate into real life actions.

An aspect of man that is difficult to change relates to his beliefs. Beliefs are deep-rooted and based on personal perceptions, which in turn springs from his environment — the things we hear, see and eat. It can be very difficult to change what we have been made to believe from childhood except a higher power is brought to bear on such beliefs. No one can change a man except the God who created him. God does this by changing his beliefs. This is often called "revelation".

Revelations could be considered as higher information or knowledge that is greater than the information upon which a man's initial beliefs were predicated or the expositions of what the ordinary mind can do ie Ezekiel, Daniel interpreting the kings dream or Joseph Gen. 41, John in the book of revelation in the Island of Patmos etc – the choice is ours as the Holy Spirit leads?. To change a belief, the information on which it is founded must change, and this can only be through a new revelation or knowledge or information.

True revelations come only from the Creator who is God. Revelations can come through a still small inner voice, through visions or dreams. In addition, we also get revelations through our contact with enlightened people who have information superior to or better than the ones we have or what we know. Revelations can also come through exposure to books, and materials from enlightened authors.

Revelations need to be clearly understood to be meaningful. If they are not properly understood, they cannot bring about any meaningful change in our beliefs. We cannot believe what we do not understand; and, understanding precedes the act of doing. Therefore revelations, understanding, and our beliefs are an essential combination that determine or propel our actions. They are elements that cannot be separated if we want a meaningful change in our lives. Our perception is also tied to them. They form the basis upon which knowledge is acquired, developed and enhanced. Therefore they are not rigid elements. They are dynamic. Hence man is described as clay that is malleable or transformable. So it is essential for us to be open-minded to be able to accept new revelations, information, new knowledge and new beliefs.

New revelation that is beneficial should be able to supplant old and unproductive ideas.

> *But the people of Berea were more open- minded than those in Thessalonica, and gladly listened to the message. They searched the Scriptures day by day to check up on Paul and Silas' statements to see if they were really so.*

Acts 17:11

Open mindedness makes listening a pleasant thing. It creates room for a true and balanced view on issues, which opens the inner ear to hear the still small voice. This invariably propels us to action. Open mindedness is a key to revelation that brings about positive change. The rigidity of a man's belief, arising from a lack of openness or sensitivity to new knowledge, can greatly hinder knowledge and consequently lead to lack of progress. Rigid people are ardent in what they believe; they are mechanical in their thinking and actions. They live in pretense rather than embrace change, even when they clearly see the unprogressive nature of such beliefs, they follow the crowd because they want to be seen "to belong" and for fear of what people might say or to avoid being put out of the synagogue (John 9; 20-23).

This was the case of the Pharisees who said to *Jesus "...we know you are a teacher who has come from God. For no one could perform the miraculous signs you are doing if God were not with him".* They knew, yet only Nicodemus had the courage to break away from the rigidity of their belief when he went, by night, to see Jesus Christ. (John 3:1-2).

Breaking away from set beliefs and accepting new knowledge that can elevate requires honest, real courage, self-examination and self-determination. Many times, we find it difficult to change our beliefs even though it is clear that such beliefs are detrimental to our progress. Rather than take conscious steps to change such beliefs, we resort to self-consolation and excuses such as 'what will be will be' or even say 'it is beyond me'. It is important that we take a hard look at our environment and situation with a view to identifying those beliefs, which are a hindrance to our progress. This has to be done sincerely until the spirit within us becomes restless, yearning for change. Until we yearn and become restless, it may be impossible to break away from retrogressive beliefs-Gen 27:40.

May this book make us restless and open- minded so that we can review our beliefs and break lose of them and get the revelations that will lead us into our inheritance!

# Sources Of Revelation

R evelation is the act of knowing or communicating divine truth. It is the divine truth that we know, believe and apply that can propel us to our inheritance. Divine truth or true revelations can come through environment, people, visions, dreams, and studying the Bible, which is the Word of God. The Bible has hidden in it revelation knowledge which honesty and openness of mind can make visible. Understanding of the written Word of God can translate the spiritual to the physical.

> *God, who at sundry times and in divers manners spake in time past unto the fathers by the prophets,*
>
> *Hath in these last days spoken unto us by his Son, whom he hath appointed heir of all things, by whom also he made the worlds;*
>
> *Who being the brightness of his glory, and the express image of his person, and upholding all things by the word of his power, when he had by himself purged our sins, sat down on the right hand of the Majesty on high;*
>
> Hebrews.1:1 – 3 (KJV)

The Bible is all about Jesus Christ, and having the accurate knowledge of Him is a revelation.

> *According as his divine power hath given unto us all things that pertain unto life and godliness, through the knowledge of him that hath called us to glory and virtue:*

> *Whereby are given unto us exceeding great and precious promises: that by these ye might be partakers of the divine nature, having escaped the corruption that is in the world through lust.*
>
> *11 Peter 1:3-4.* (KJV)

An open-minded man may understand the things of God better, because God has made things plain to everyone who has an open mind and is willing to listen and obey. As the Bible says:

> *For since the creation of the world God's invisible qualities-his eternal power and divine nature-have been clearly seen, being understood from what has been made, so that men are without excuse.*
>
> Romans 1:20

A careful observation of what God has created gives insight to the revelation of God, His method of operation, and what He wants man to know; how to live and what to do. Understanding nature and relating it to Jesus Christ and to life situations is revelation.

This also has to do with our perception and understanding of nature. How do we see nature and its different characteristics? How have we related them to the knowledge and understanding of God and His ways of operation? Most things we want to know about God can be found hidden in the things He has created and revealed to who so ever truly desires to know. This is known as general revelation.

The Bible expressly states that *"...secret things belong to the LORD our God, but the things revealed belong to us and to our children forever, that we may follow all the words of this law."* (Deuteronomy 29:29).

Things have already been revealed. Nature has hidden revelations concerning God and His ways of operation. Studying nature alone can reveal a great deal about the characteristics of God, and a proper analysis of those characteristics would show how God wants people to behave or conduct themselves here on earth, the temporal abode of man. Nothing happens outside its season and time. Things just do not happen! Everything goes through a process, and every process has a beginning and an ending. So until the fullness of time no result may be achieved. There is a time for everything. Therefore knowing the right timing for an activity enables us to get the right result, whether we prayed or not; whether we believed or not. Results have to do with "doing the right thing at the right time". Conversely, if we do the right thing at the wrong time whether we prayed or not, we will get the wrong result. This illustrates that God has put certain laws in place such that whether we believed these laws or not such laws are binding. Revelations from God is still available, like in the days of the old, but most people are not open-minded enough to listen, observe and apply such revelations. The deceptiveness and wickedness of man has greatly hindered Godly perception. Humanity is suspicious of humanity. Pressures that abound in the world have hardened the heart of man, 'deafening and blinding' both his inner ear and eye. It is written:

> *And God said, Let us make man in our image, after our likeness: and let them have dominion over the fish of the sea, and over the fowl of the air, and over the cattle, and over all the earth, and over every creeping thing that creepeth upon the earth.*
>
> *So God created man in his own image, in the image of God created he him; male and female created he them.*
>
> *And God blessed them, and God said unto them, Be fruitful, and multiply, and replenish the earth, and subdue it: and have dominion over the fish of the sea, and over the fowl of the air, and over every living thing that moveth upon the earth.*
>
> *Genesis 1:26—28 (KJV)*

Even the intellect that God gave man to know and work with Him has now become a hindrance to receiving true revelation from Him, because of sin. Some men reason that they are wiser than God. Some scientists think they are wiser than God or at least try to equate themselves with God as far as creation and knowledge is concerned. Yet the Bible says:

> *But God chose the foolish things of the world to shame the wise; God chose the weak things of the world to shame the strong. He chose the lowly things of this world and the despised things-and the things that are not-to nullify the things that are, so that no one may boast before hint.*

*1Corinthians 1:27-29*

Furthermore, it is written:

> *For my thoughts are not your thoughts, neither are your ways my ways, saith the LORD.*
>
> *For as the heavens are higher than the earth, so are my ways higher than your ways, and my thoughts than your thoughts.*

Isaiah 55:8—9 (KJV)

We require open-mindedness, commitment; submission and obedience to God to get true revelation. God is ever ready to reveal Himself to all who genuinely desire to know Him. Jesus says:

> *Come unto me, all ye that labour and are heavy laden, and I will give you rest.*
>
> *Take my yoke upon you, and learn of me; for I am meek and lowly in heart: and ye shall find rest unto your souls.*
>
> *For my yoke is easy, and my burden is light*

Matthew 11:28-30 (KJV)

But we must be humble and gentle, and seek Him with a purposeful heart - a heart that is supple or flexible. God's desire to reveal Himself to the sons and daughters of men is made expressly manifest in Scripture:

*And I say unto you, Ask, and it shall be given you; seek, and ye shall find; knock, and it shall be opened unto you. 10 For every one that asketh receiveth; and he that seeketh findeth; and to him that knocketh it shall be opened.*

*Luke 11:9-10 (KJV)*

*He called a little child and had him stand among them. And he said: "I tell you the truth, unless you change and become like little children, you will never enter the kingdom of heaven.*

*Therefore, whoever humbles himself like this child is the greatest in the kingdom of heaven.*

*Matthew 18:2-4*

The most genuine revelations can be obtained from the Bible, which is the Word of God. God and His Word are one. God honours His Word above His Name. We can get or confirm true revelations from the Word of God if we are open-minded, have an honest, flexible perception and have the Spirit of God. We cannot get this Spirit of God if we are not born- again. The Spirit of God reveals all things and He Himself (the Holy Spirit) has been given to all who believe in Jesus Christ as the Son of the living God who came in flesh and blood and was crucified for our sins.

*And there were dwelling at Jerusalem Jews, devout men, out of every nation under heaven.*

*Now when this was noised abroad, the multitude came together, and were confounded, because that every man heard them speak in his own language.*

*And they were all amazed and marveled, saying one to another, Behold, are not all these which speak Galileans?*

*And how hear we every man in our own tongue, wherein we were born?*

*Parthians, and Medes, and Elamites, and the dwellers in Mesopotamia, and in Judaea, and Cappadocia, in Pontus, and Asia,*

*Phrygia, and Pamphylia, in Egypt, and in the parts of Libya about Cyrene, and strangers of Rome, Jews and proselytes,*

*Cretes and Arabians, we do hear them speak in our tongues the wonderful works of God.*

*And they were all amazed, and were in doubt, saying one to another, What meaneth this?*

*Others mocking said, These men are full of new wine.*

*But Peter, standing up with the eleven, lifted up his voice, and said unto them, Ye men of Judaea, and all ye that dwell at Jerusalem, be this known unto you, and hearken to my words:*

*For these are not drunken, as ye suppose, seeing it is but the third hour of the day.*

*But this is that which was spoken by the prophet Joel;*

*And it shall come to pass in the last days, saith God, I will pour out of my Spirit upon all flesh: and your sons and your daughters shall prophesy, and your young men shall see visions, and your old men shall dream dreams:*

*And on my servants and on my handmaidens I will pour out in those days of my Spirit; and they shall prophesy:*

*And I will shew wonders in heaven above, and signs in the earth beneath; blood, and fire, and vapour of smoke:*

*The sun shall be turned into darkness, and the moon into blood, before that great and notable day of the Lord come:*

*And it shall come to pass, that whosoever shall call on the name of the Lord shall be saved.*

*Acts 2:5-21 (KJV)*

Revelations are true, and they abound to this day. Knowing truth is revelations, John 8:32. Of course, fake ones also exist. True revelations co-exist with the false or fake ones, Mat 13:30. It is with the help of the Spirit of God that we are able to differentiate the true from the fake one. Maturity in handling the things of God is primary to our ability to decipher true revelation from the fake. We can also identify fake revelations by their fruit.

> *Another parable put he forth unto them, saying, The kingdom of heaven is likened unto a man which sowed good seed in his field:*
>
> *But while men slept, his enemy came and sowed tares among the wheat, and went his way.*
>
> *But when the blade was sprung up, and brought forth fruit, then appeared the tares also.*
>
> *So the servants of the householder came and said unto him, Sir, didst not thou sow good seed in thy field? from whence then hath it tares?*
>
> *He said unto them, An enemy hath done this. The servants said unto him, Wilt thou then that we go and gather them up?*
>
> *But he said, Nay; lest while ye gather up the tares, ye root up also the wheat with them.*
>
> *Let both grow together until the harvest: and in the time of harvest I will say to the reapers, Gather ye together first the tares, and bind them in bundles to burn them: but gather the wheat into my barn.*
>
> *Matthew 13:24-30 (KJV)*

# The Word Of God

The Word of God has a voice and can be audible to those who desire to hear. It can be a still, small inner voice to those who want to listen. It can be read and understood from the Bible by those who study with appreciable measure of openness of heart. Through dreams, visions, genuine Christian friends and spiritual leaders, people also get to hear the word of God. We need to understand and fully accept that God is God! And as God, He can do whatever He wants to do by whatever means, at whatever time and place. He used ravens to feed Elijah (1Kings 17:6). God stands out all by Himself. Therefore He can decide to speak to us by whatever means. We do not decide the means and ways for Him to use. He is simply God. After all He spoke through a donkey to Balaam (Numbers 22:28) and to Elijah directly 1 Kings 19:11-14; to Moses it was face-to-face as a friend Numbers 12:6-8.

Therefore, anyone desirous of hearing God would need to be flexible and sensitive because there is no telling what direction He might visit from. Generally, His Words bring peace, comfort and hope to those who hear them. They are never hasty as to coerce us to be worried or afraid. God is still in the business of speaking to those who care to listen and in fact He clearly spoke through Jesus Christ who is His very image. The question is: how do we perceive the Word of God spoken either audibly, written or through vision, revelations or even through friends and spiritual leaders?

How we perceive the Word of God or His voice will greatly determine what revelations we get. The type of revelation obtainable will determine the preparations we may be required to make in order to receive the benefits. Sometimes a wrong mind-set or perception will make us get nothing at all. Perception goes a long way in determining how we study, listen and understand. Many people spend their time 'tarrying' because they want to see the heavens open and desire to hear a loud voice saying, "this is God" or "this is what He wants us to know, say or do". This may never happen. People who expect such events may die in their ignorant expectations. They are firmly set in the mode and manner they expect God to speak to them. They are unwilling to know that there could be other ways through which God speaks, therefore refuse to hear by any means different from what they expect.

People have various names by which they describe or call the Bible or the Word of God. What we call the Bible will determine how we will see or perceive it, which will in turn greatly determine or influence what we make of it. To some people the Bible is a mere story book. For such people, it cannot be any other thing, but a book of good fiction suitable for nothing but amusement. That is why we have some theologians and professors-emeritus of the Bible, who get no revelation from it that can change their lives. They see it as a mere tool for lecturing and as a means of livelihood. The Pharisees, the Sadducees and the Teachers of the Law deprived themselves of the benefits that accrued to those who believe in the Word of God. During the earthly ministry of Jesus Christ, they depended on their work of self- righteousness and in the process, missed out on the power of God. See the encounter of Nicodemus with Jesus:

> *There was a man of the Pharisees, named Nicodemus, a ruler of the Jews:*
>
> *The same came to Jesus by night, and said unto him, Rabbi, we know that thou art a teacher come from God: for no man can do these miracles that thou doest, except God be with him.*
>
> *Jesus answered and said unto him, Verily, verily, I say unto thee, Except a man be born again, he cannot see the kingdom of God.*
>
> *Nicodemus saith unto him, How can a man be born when he is old? can he enter the second time into his mother's womb, and be born?*

*Jesus answered, Verily, verily, I say unto thee, Except a man be born of water and of the Spirit, he cannot enter into the kingdom of God.*

*That which is born of the flesh is flesh; and that which is born of the Spirit is spirit.*

*Marvel not that I said unto thee, Ye must be born again.*

*The wind bloweth where it listeth, and thou hearest the sound thereof, but canst not tell whence it cometh, and whither it goeth: so is every one that is born of the Spirit.*

*Nicodemus answered and said unto him, How can these things be?*

*Jesus answered and said unto him, Art thou a master of Israel, and knowest not these things?*

*Verily, verily, I say unto thee, We speak that we do know, and testify that we have seen; and ye receive not our witness.*

*If I have told you earthly things, and ye believe not, how shall ye believe, if I tell you of heavenly things?*

*And no man hath ascended up to heaven, but he that came down from heaven, even the Son of man which is in heaven.*

*And as Moses lifted up the serpent in the wilderness, even so must the Son of man be lifted up:*

*That whosoever believeth in him should not perish, but have eternal life.*

*John 3:1—15 (KJV)*

Some see the written Word of God - the Bible as a challenge to their intellect or an infringement upon their authority. See what King Herod did:

*Now when Jesus was born in Bethlehem of Judaea in the days of Herod the king, behold, there came wise men from the east to Jerusalem,*

*Saying, Where is he that is born King of the Jews? for we have seen his star in the east, and are come to worship him.*

*When Herod the king had heard these things, he was troubled, and all Jerusalem with him.*

*And when he had gathered all the chief priests and scribes of the people together, he demanded of them where Christ should be born.*

*And they said unto him, In Bethlehem of Judaea: for thus it is written by the prophet,*

*And thou Bethlehem, in the land of Juda, art not the least among the princes of Juda: for out of thee shall come a Governor, that shall rule my people Israel.*

*Matthew 2:1—6 (KJV)*

The Word of God does not benefit such people as they have no revelation and have no expectation. They remain dejected and miserable until death crushes them. They spend their lives fighting the One they cannot defeat — the One who formed them from a mould of clay.

Some others see the Word of God only as a mere book of promises as indeed it is as children of Abraham but forget the caveats. This set of people are like children walking into Santa- Claus's booth to collect a gift pack. How wonderful it would have been were it that easy and for us to be children forever! If it were so, the world would have been filled with lots of blessings;' lots of fulfilled promises! These are the people who do funny things- most of them unbelievable. They claim the Word for every situation they find themselves. They expect a miracle to take place. They spend their lives claiming one promise after another, yet their lives remain the same or even become worse. When they eventually realize that it is not working, they resort to self-consolation, the exoneration of their foolishness by blaming someone else, especially the devil. This is foolish faith. After all faith and works go together. Look at the seven Sons of Sceva:

*Some Jews who went around driving out evil spirits tried to invoke the name of the Lord Jesus over those who were* demon-possessed. *They would say, "In the name of Jesus, whom Paul preaches, I command you to come out." Seven sons of Sceva, a Jewish chief priest, were doing this. [One day] the evil spirit answered them, "Jesus I know, and I know about Paul, but who are you?" Then the man who had the evil spirit jumped on them and overpowered them all. He gave them such a beating that they ran out of the house naked and bleeding.*

Acts 19:13—16

This kind of word claiming may be tantamount to invocation, which is sin before God. It does not work.

Some see the Word of God as a contract document and as such have the mindset of an offer and an acceptance with the intention of creating a legal relationship, which is enforceable in the event of a breach. This set of people study the Bible to know or clearly identify the offer, in order to decide whether to accept or not to accept because of the consequences of a breach or whether it will be profitable or not. They want to know, understand all their rights and obligations before they can accept the offer. Were God to tell this kind of people to leave their households and go to a place he would show them, as He told Abraham, they would want to know why they must leave, where they are going and what will be the benefits? They would surely want to make sure that everything lines up with their understanding and plans before they make or take a decision. To these people whatever is not clear can either wait or is not acceptable. They are very slow to believe because their understanding is restricted to their own head knowledge. They work outside faith.

*The LORD had said to Abram, Leave your country, your people and your father's household and go to the land I will show you. "I will make you into a great nation and I will bless you; I will make your name great, and you will be a blessing. I will bless those who bless you, and whoever curses you I will curse; and all peoples on earth will be blessed through you.*

Genesis 12:1—3

Others see the Word of God as a legal document. They study it only to get out and develop a set of rigid laws-"Thou shall not". This set of people compile rules of "dos and don'ts" which must not be tampered with. If you go against anything, the penalty is excommunication or outright death. The story of the woman caught in adultery illustrates this aptly:

> *And the scribes and Pharisees brought unto him a woman taken in adultery; and when they had set her in the midst,*
>
> *They say unto him, Master, this woman was taken in adultery, in the very act.*
>
> *Now Moses in the law commanded us, that such should be stoned: but what sayest thou?*
>
> *This they said, tempting him, that they might have to accuse him. But Jesus stooped down, and with his finger wrote on the ground, as though he heard them not.*
>
> *So when they continued asking him, he lifted up himself, and said unto them, He that is without sin among you, let him first cast a stone at her.*
>
> *And again he stooped down, and wrote on the ground.*
>
> *And they which heard it, being convicted by their own conscience, went out one by one, beginning at the eldest, even unto the last: and Jesus was left alone, and the woman standing in the midst.*
>
> *When Jesus had lifted up himself, and saw none but the woman, he said unto her, Woman, where are those thine accusers? hath no man condemned thee?*
>
> *She said, No man, Lord. And Jesus said unto her, Neither do I condemn thee: go, and sin no more.*
>
> *John 8:3—11 (KJV)*

These categories of people do not give or allow room for mistakes, which could lead to better knowledge and growth. They cage people's freedom to express their individual opinions: such an ambience is of intense fear and pretense. It builds false righteousness. Their actions do not really express their inner being. The outside of the cup is pure white but the inner part or even the content is rotten. They have a rigid mindset -"This is what we know and nothing else". They hear but do not believe. They see but do not perceive. Their hearts are hardened by their mindset. They have rocky-soil types of hearts. These are the ones who stir up dissension in the assembly of saints especially when there is any change; or they are denied exalted or front seats and titles in the church. They are merciless, as they are fault-finders. They go against miracles and forgiveness. They are quick to assert "the soul that sins must die". They are the ones that would shout "crucify him; crucify him". They claim to know God but by their actions deny Him (Titus 1:16).

The Lord Jesus described people of this disposition as follows:

> *Woe unto you, scribes and Pharisees, hypocrites! for ye make clean the outside of the cup and of the platter, but within they are full of extortion and excess.*

> *Thou blind Pharisee, cleanse first that which is within the cup and platter that the outside of them may be clean also.*

> *Woe unto you, scribes and Pharisees, hypocrites! for ye are like unto whited sepulchres, which indeed appear beautiful outward, but are within full of dead men's bones, and of all uncleanness.*

> *Even so ye also outwardly appear righteous unto men, but within ye are full of hypocrisy and iniquity.*

> *Woe unto you, scribes and Pharisees, hypocrites! because ye build the tombs of the prophets, and garnish the sepulchres of the righteous,*

> *And say, If we had been in the days of our fathers, we would not have been partakers with them in the blood of the prophets.*

> *Wherefore ye be witnesses unto yourselves, that ye are the children of them which killed the prophets.*

*Fill ye up then the measure of your fathers.*

*Matthew 23:25—32 (KJV)*

There are also those who take the Word of God as a book of Godly treasures that can be accessed through faith. These are the people with an open mindset. They search the Bible with an open mind, to search out the principles of accessing and getting out the treasures God has promised. They learn, train themselves in the principles, nurture, and believe them. They act upon the Word by faith. They have a supple or flexible mindset. They are described as "clay-minded" people. They believe that the Word of God is like a seed that must be sown and allowed to grow and bear fruit. They believe that knowledge is not rigid; learning has no end. They know that every principle must go through a process and every process has a beginning and an end so they patiently wait to see or get to the end like the farmer, having done his part, waits patiently for harvest. They listen and accept superior reasoning or argument. When what they know is not yielding any positive result to cause change for others to notice and comment they seek new information desperately from God. They are objective and true to themselves. They know that faith often does not make sense to humans. They allow their human intellect to die. They are the ones whose hearts are the fertile soil.

> "But the people of Berea were more open- minded than
> those in Thessalonica, and gladly listened to the message.
> They searched the Scriptures day by day to check up on
> Paul and Silas' statements to see if they were really so"
>
> Acts 17:11

Then there are those who call themselves "freethinkers". They don't belong to any of the classes above, and they say there is no God. They are "fools". They are carefree. To them, what is, has been; and what will be, will be." Again it is important to note, nothing just happens for the sake of happening. These people are living a life based on assumption. Nothing on this part of life is neutral, or just happens. We are either for or against God. These various kinds of people and their disposition to information or knowledge, based on their mind set is' what our Lord and Saviour Jesus Christ generally described in the Gospel according to St. Matthew with the parable of the sower.

> *The same day went Jesus out of the house, and sat by the sea side.*
>
> *And great multitudes were gathered together unto him, so that he went into a ship, and sat; and the whole multitude stood on the shore.*
>
> *And he spake many things unto them in parables, saying, Behold, a sower went forth to sow;*
>
> *And when he sowed, some seeds fell by the way side, and the fowls came and devoured them up:*
>
> *Some fell upon stony places, where they had not much earth: and forthwith they sprung up, because they had no deepness of earth:*
>
> *And when the sun was up, they were scorched; and because they had no root, they withered away.*
>
> *And some fell among thorns; and the thorns sprung up, and choked them:*
>
> *But other fell into good ground, and brought forth fruit, some an hundredfold, some sixtyfold, some thirtyfold.*
>
> *Who hath ears to hear, let him hear.*
>
> *And the disciples came, and said unto him, Why speakest thou unto them in parables?*
>
> *He answered and said unto them, Because it is given unto you to know the mysteries of the kingdom of heaven, but to them it is not given.*
>
> *For whosoever hath, to him shall be given, and he shall have more abundance: but whosoever hath not, from him shall be taken away even that he hath.*

*Therefore speak I to them in parables: because they seeing see not; and hearing they hear not, neither do they understand.*

*And in them is fulfilled the prophecy of Esaias, which saith, By hearing ye shall hear, and shall not understand; and seeing ye shall see, and shall not perceive:*

*For this people's heart is waxed gross, and their ears are dull of hearing, and their eyes they have closed; lest at any time they should see with their eyes, and hear with their ears, and should understand with their heart, and should be converted, and I should heal them.*

*But blessed are your eyes, for they see: and your ears, for they hear.*

*For verily I say unto you, That many prophets and righteous men have desired to see those things which ye see, and have not seen them; and to hear those things which ye hear, and have not heard them.*

*Hear ye therefore the parable of the sower.*

*When any one heareth the word of the kingdom, and understandeth it not, then cometh the wicked one, and catcheth away that which was sown in his heart. This is he which received seed by the way side.*

*But he that received the seed into stony places, the same is he that heareth the word, and anon with joy receiveth it;*

*Yet hath he not root in himself, but dureth for a while: for when tribulation or persecution ariseth because of the word, by and by he is offended.*

*He also that received seed among the thorns is he that heareth the word; and the care of this world, and the deceitfulness of riches, choke the word, and he becometh unfruitful.*

*But he that received seed into the good ground is he that heareth the word, and understandeth it; which also beareth fruit, and bringeth forth, some an hundredfold, some sixty, some thirty.*

*Matthew 13:1—23 (KJV)*

This goes to explain that studying the scriptures and or merely listening to messages on salvation or eternal life does not give us salvation or eternal life. We must study the scriptures or listen to the gospel messages, understand them, be convicted and be able to receive the gift of salvation or eternal life for ourselves, by ourselves and through faith in Christ Jesus.

*In the first year of Darius son of Xerxes (a Mede by descent), who was made ruler over the Babylonian kingdom - in the first year of his reign, I, Daniel, understood from the Scriptures, according to the word of the LORD given to Jeremiah the prophet, that the desolation of Jerusalem would last seventy years. So I turned to the Lord God and pleaded with him in prayer and petition, in fasting, and in sackcloth and ashes*

Daniel 9:1—3

*"You diligently study the Scriptures because you think that by them you possess eternal life. These are the Scriptures that testify about me, yet you refuse to come to me to have life"*

John 5:39-40

The Jews of old lacked the kind of understanding that Daniel had. Most times, people misunderstand what Jesus meant when He said:

*"The thief comes only to steal and kill and destroy; I have come that they may have life, and have it to the full"*

John 10:10

24

The thief is the devil. He is a spirit and therefore does not come to steal our goats, cars or houses directly because he does not need them. What he comes to steal is the information we have concerning salvation or eternal life that we do not understand (Mat 13:19). Salvation means everything we need for good life and godliness; and eternal life means life after life: life in union with God forever. It is the knowledge of God and His son, Jesus Christ (John 17:3). God does not give us money or houses, and so forth directly, what He does is give us the requisite information or ideas or the ability to do through His word so that we can obtain the aforementioned. He says, "I send forth my Word and it heals" Psalm 107:20 and Deut 8:18. It is this Word that the devil attempts to steal but he cannot steal all the information we have concerning salvation or eternal life. He can only steal the ones for which we do not have full understanding to believe and do. People from whom he steals such information are those who prove to have no root. For those he cannot steal from, he attempts to distort the information available to them so as to confuse them. What we know, understand, believe and constantly do by an act of faith becomes a part of us. It is exceedingly difficult to steal or distort something that is already a part of us. This is why the enemy - the devil, finds it very difficult to tempt us in areas where we have had genuine experience or encounter of victory. What we have honestly and methodically conquered will always be subject to our control. Jesus Christ conquered the devil and death once and for all, and they shall forever be subject to His control. The devil goes to and fro looking for whom to devour. This means he cannot devour everyone, and that is why he is looking. He is looking for those who do not have an in-depth understanding of what they believe and who do not do what they believe. To overcome the devil we must gain proper understanding and become a doer of the Word, to gain victory to become a conqueror. We are only conquerors over what we have overcome. Therefore we must not avoid situations that hinder us, but confront, overtake and conquer, to make subject to us.

# God Is Mighty

We need to really understand who God is. He is the Almighty God, He is the creator: He is the All-Powerful. He can do and undo. Beside Him there is no other. He does whatever pleases Him (Job 23:13), by whatever means and at whatever place. This is why He is God. At creation, He said, "*let there be*" and it was so. Since then God has never had to again use those words: "*let there be*". From then everything God made became a tool in His hand. Tools are for use and not for mere decoration. God being God can use anything or person to achieve His purpose. He can do anything at any time and place. Therefore we are all vessels in His hand.

Once upon a time He spoke through a donkey to convey a message. The Bible records:

> *And Balaam rose up in the morning, and saddled his ass, and went with the princes of Moab.*
>
> *And God's anger was kindled because he went: and the angel of the LORD stood in the way for an adversary against him. Now he was riding upon his ass, and his two servants were with him.*
>
> *And the ass saw the angel of the LORD standing in the way, and his sword drawn in his hand: and the ass turned aside out of the way, and went into the field: and Balaam smote the ass, to turn her into the way.*
>
> *But the angel of the LORD stood in a path of the vineyards, a wall being on this side, and a wall on that side.*

*And when the ass saw the angel of the LORD, she thrust herself unto the wall, and crushed Balaam's foot against the wall: and he smote her again.*

*And the angel of the LORD went further, and stood in a narrow place, where was no way to turn either to the right hand or to the left.*

*And when the ass saw the angel of the LORD, she fell down under Balaam: and Balaam's anger was kindled, and he smote the ass with a staff.*

*And the LORD opened the mouth of the ass, and she said unto Balaam, What have I done unto thee, that thou hast smitten me these three times?*

*And Balaam said unto the ass, Because thou hast mocked me: I would there were a sword in mine hand, for now would I kill thee.*

*And the ass said unto Balaam, Am not I thine ass, upon which thou hast ridden ever since I was thine unto this day? Was I ever wont to do so unto thee? And he said, Nay.*

*Then the LORD opened the eyes of Balaam, and he saw the angel of the LORD standing in the way, and his sword drawn in his hand: and he bowed down his head, and fell flat on his face.*

*And the angel of the LORD said unto him, Wherefore hast thou smitten thine ass these three times? behold, I went out to withstand thee, because thy way is perverse before me:*

*And the ass saw me, and turned from me these three times: unless she had turned from me, surely now also I had slain thee, and saved her alive.*

*Numbers 22:21-33 (KJV)*

God is to be feared. On another occasion He sent food to Elijah through the ravens.

> *And Elijah the Tishbite, who was of the inhabitants of Gilead, said unto Ahab, As the LORD God of Israel liveth, before whom I stand, there shall not be dew nor rain these years, but according to my word.*
>
> *And the word of the LORD came unto him, saying,*
>
> *Get thee hence, and turn thee eastward, and hide thyself by the brook Cherith, that is before Jordan.*
>
> *And it shall be, that thou shalt drink of the brook; and I have commanded the ravens to feed thee there.*
>
> *So he went and did according unto the word of the LORD: for he went and dwelt by the brook Cherith, that is before Jordan.*
>
> *And the ravens brought him bread and flesh in the morning, and bread and flesh in the evening; and he drank of the brook.*
>
> *1Kings 17:1-6 (KJV)*

The Israelites were at a certain time in a great dilemma. Before them was the Red Sea, on both sides were mountains and behind them were their enemies; the Egyptians, who were pursuing to kill them. This would have given God the opportunity to say, "*let this or that happen.*" He did not. Rather He' said to Moses "what is that you have in your hand; use it". He used what was in the hand of Moses. The Bible says:

> *As Pharaoh approached, the Israelites looked up, and there were the Egyptians, marching after them. They were terrified and cried out to the LORD. They said to Moses, "Was it because there were no graves in Egypt that you brought us to the desert to die? what have you done to us by bringing us out of Egypt? Didn't we say to you in Egypt, 'Leave us alone; let us serve the Egyptians'? It would have*

*been better for us to serve the Egyptians than to die in the desert!" Moses answered the people "Do not be afraid. Stand firm and you will see the deliverance the LORD will bring you today. The Egyptians you see today you will never see again. The LORD will fight for you; need only to be still." Then the LORD said to Moses, "Why are you crying out to me? Tell the Israelites to move on. Raise your staff and stretch out your hand over the sea to divide the water so that the Israelites can go through the sea on dry ground.*

Exodus 14:10-17

This is also the case when we trivialize or neglect certain Words of God said to us through our spiritual leaders. Because we only desire to hear God the way we want Him to speak to us. We most probably will continue watching and waiting until we perish. Meanwhile He could have spoken through His own chosen methods. We must know that God is at liberty to do anything, by whatever methods, to achieve His purpose, which is of paramount importance to Him. If we can understand and believe this, then we will know that we need to be more sensitive to what happens with and in us. Nothing that happens to us is ever ordinary or surprising to God. This is why it is very important for us to be personally convinced and convicted about issues of life than rely on only what other people tell us about them. What we tell ourselves in conviction does help us withstand the challenges of life. In the same vein, we oftentimes want God to answer our prayers through our own methods. Sometimes we tell Him what to do and how to do it. If He does this, why is He God? We have been expecting Him to act from the wrong direction or we want to receive things from the wrong direction. Our directions and ways are usually too complex and burdensome, and so we put yokes on ourselves that we cannot bear. This could be the reason why we cannot do most things we tell other people to do. Simply put, *"do what I say but not what I do"*. We find it difficult to live out what we tell others to do. This is what Jesus Christ accused the teachers of the law and the Pharisees of in Matthew 23. We confidently say to ourselves, "this is not God but a man like me. He is just privileged to be my spiritual leader". If we must hear God the way we want to hear Him we just might keep watching and waiting until we perish while God could have spoken through His own methods.

> *And Miriam and Aaron spake against Moses because of the Ethiopian woman whom he had married: for he had married an Ethiopian woman.*
>
> *And they said, Hath the LORD indeed spoken only by Moses? hath he not spoken also by us? And the LORD heard it.*
>
> *Numbers 12:1-2 (KJV)*
>
> *And the apostles and elders came together for to consider of this matter. And when there had been much disputing, Peter rose up, and said unto them, Men and brethren, ye know how that a good while ago God made choice among us, that the Gentiles by my mouth should hear the word of the gospel, and believe.*
>
> *And God, which knoweth the hearts, bare them witness, giving them the Holy Ghost, even as he did unto us;*
>
> *And put no difference between us and them, purifying their hearts by faith.*
>
> *Now therefore why tempt ye God, to put a yoke upon the neck of the disciples, which neither our fathers nor we were able to bear?*
>
> *But we believe that through the grace of the Lord Jesus Christ we shall be saved, even as they.*
>
> *Acts 15:6-11 (KJV)*

All we require to do is to tell God the problem, and how He does it, is best known to Him. The Word of God is not complex just as His ways are not complex. Sin brought in complexity and since then man has become too complex and finds it difficult to keep simple in his ways. It is termed "sophistication". Some would go to the extent of seeking scientific proof for everything before they can believe. When something becomes too simple it tends to be unreal to the human understanding. This is the challenge of Christianity today — simplicity! Christianity appears too simple to be true and yet it is true indeed. The fact is aptly illustrated by the story of Naaman:

> *Now Naaman, captain of the host of the king of Syria, was a great man with his master, and honourable, because by him the LORD had given deliverance unto Syria: he was also a mighty man in valour, but he was a leper.*

> *And the Syrians had gone out by companies, and had brought away captive out of the land of Israel a little maid; and she waited on Naaman's wife.*

> *And she said unto her mistress, Would God my lord were with the prophet that is in Samaria! for he would recover him of his leprosy.*

> *And one went in, and told his lord, saying, Thus and thus said the maid that is of the land of Israel.*

> *And the king of Syria said, Go to, go, and I will send a letter unto the king of Israel. And he departed, and took with him ten talents of silver, and six thousand pieces of gold, and ten changes of raiment.*

> *And he brought the letter to the king of Israel, saying, Now when this letter is come unto thee, behold, I have therewith sent Naaman my servant to thee, that thou mayest recover him of his leprosy.*

> *And it came to pass, when the king of Israel had read the letter, that he rent his clothes, and said, Am I God, to kill and to make alive, that this man doth send unto me to recover a man of his leprosy? wherefore consider, I pray you, and see how he seeketh a quarrel against me.*

> *And it was so, when Elisha the man of God had heard that the king of Israel had rent his clothes, that he sent*

*to the king, saying, Wherefore hast thou rent thy clothes? let him come now to me, and he shall know that there is a prophet in Israel.*

*So Naaman came with his horses and with his chariot, and stood at the door of the house of Elisha.*

*And Elisha sent a messenger unto him, saying, Go and wash in the Jordan seven times, and thy flesh shall come again to thee, and thou shalt be clean.*

*But Naaman was wroth, and went away, and said, Behold, I thought, He will surely come out to me, and stand, and call on the name of the LORD his God, and strike his hand over the place, and recover the leper.*

*Are not Abana and Pharpar, rivers of Damascus, better than all the waters of Israel? may I not wash in them, and be clean? So he turned and went away in a rage.*

*And his servants came near, and spake unto him, and said, My father, if the prophet had bid thee do some great thing, wouldest thou not have done it? how much rather then, when he saith to thee, Wash, and be clean?*

*Then went he down, and dipped himself seven times in Jordan, according to the saying of the man of God: and his flesh came again like unto the flesh of a little child, and he was clean.*

*2 Kings 5:1 —14 (KJV)*

Our mind has been conditioned by sin to appreciate things better when they are complex and expensive. Once we make a thing free and cheap it seems to lose value. We therefore have fashioned a myth to make God's simple Word complex in order to give it value and acceptance, thereby conforming to our standard. We need to shift from this paradigm if we want to enjoy the full benefits of the Word of God. Some humble Church leaders are scarcely regarded by people because they appear not "deep enough". The people of this age are in a frantic search for the 'supposed' deep things of God, but their methods unwittingly throw them into the hands of the devil. The complexities that we want the Word of God to be before we believe have brought more division and confusion into Christendom than ever before. I remember working for several years without promotion. I decided to fast and pray for a season. Then, one morning, after my prayer, I heard a voice from God saying, "Go tell your boss to promote you". "Is it this simple?" I asked myself, struggling with the thought of going to tell my boss to promote me as was directed. The more I tried to drown this supposedly self- imposed thought, the more I wanted to try it out. Finally, I began to put together documents, letters, memos and certificates, in preparation to making a good case for my promotion, which, was over-due. I spent time to rehearse my presentations until the day came. I remember that morning very clearly; as I hauled the huge box file along the corridor to my boss's office, ready to counter whatever arguments might arise. I walked into the office determined to win every argument. I cannot remember if my boss noticed my huge box file which I never made reference to. As I walked into my boss's office, he asked me what the matter was. I said, "Sir, promote me". He threw glances about for a while, and said to me, 'Okay. You are promoted. Go." I was stunned, speechless and wondered in disbelief as I left his office, but the next day I received a letter confirming my promotion. The heavy box file I burdened myself to put together and spent energy to carry was never used. God's Word is simple just like' His ways are mighty. No wonder a writer said, "If we shape ourselves according to nature, we will never be poor, but if we shape ourselves according to people's demand, we will never be rich. This is because what nature demands is easy and simple but people's demands can be complex and burdensome. We can never please people's opinion". As Jesus once said:

> "For John came neither eating nor drinking, and they say, 'He has a demon.' The Son of Man came eating and drinking, and they say, 'Here is a glutton and a drunkard, a friend of tax collectors and "sinners."'But wisdom is proved right by her actions"

> Matthew 11:18-19

As my boss never noticed my heavy box file so it is with many of us who try to be complex in carrying out simple instructions. **The moment we hear God's voice or receive His Word, the only thing we need to do is just believe, trust, accept and obey - whether it is meaningful to us or not.** Sometimes we may not need any preparation, 'just' simple obedience of "doing". That is God's requirement from us - *"just"* simple obedience. He is God Almighty. He watches over His instructions to perform them. As the song writer says... *trust and obey, there's no other way to be happy in Jesus but to trust and obey.*

Some people reject the gift of salvation, which Jesus obtained on their behalf with His precious blood because they consider the sinners prayer that is required for salvation too simple. For such people, it is unbelievable that we can be saved by simply praying: *"Dear Lord Jesus, I confess with my mouth that I am a sinner. I confess that I cannot save myself. Have mercy on me and cleanse me with your blood from all my unrighteousness. Come into my life and be my Lord and Saviour. Put my name in your book of life. From today I am born again. No matter the sin we must have committed this simple prayer makes us totally forgiven reconciling us to God.* This reconciliation is called "true life" or "true living". This is considered too ridiculously simple to be real and so many lose out on eternal life. Naaman's servant asked him, "Had the man of God told you to do a complex thing would you not have done it?" If Naaman had neglected that advice, he would have died a miserable and repulsive leper. Truly, God's Word is real and simple.

> *"For the word of God is living and active. Sharper than any double-edged sword, it penetrates even to dividing soul and spirit, joints and marrow; it judges the thoughts and attitudes of the heart"*

> Hebrews 4:12

People need to clearly understand that God is God. He is one with His Word. He is mighty and can do whatever He wants to do without seeking any permission or apology from anyone. His Words are mighty; cannot be chained, and cannot return to Him without accomplishing its purpose; therefore it will carry out and complete what it was supposed to do. Nothing can contend with God or His Word. He is the One who diligently rewards, protects, defends and avenges those who seek and depend on Him. He is the One who will never leave us or forsake us no matter what. When we go through the fire He is with us. When we pass through the waters it will not drown us. He is the ever-present help in times of trouble. Examples abound: Remember the deliverance of the Israelites from Egypt and the plagues God unleashed on that land to obtain that deliverance? (Exodus 8-11). Remember the crossing of the Red Sea? (Exodus 14:13-19). Remember the three Hebrew boys that were thrown in the furnace of fire or Daniel in the lion's den? (Daniel 4-6).

King Nebuchadnezzar saw God's greatness and declared in Daniel 4:1-3 *"...How great are His signs, how mighty His wonders! His kingdom is an eternal kingdom; His dominion endures from generation to generation"*.

King Darius saw His awesomeness and issued a decree in Daniel 7: 25-27 *"...He is the living God and He endures forever; His kingdom will not be destroyed, His dominion will never end. He rescues and saves; He performs signs and wonders in the heavens and on the earth. He has rescued Daniel from the power of the lions"*.

*Moses wrote about Him:*

> *"Then I pleaded with the LORD at that time, saying: 'O Lord GOD, You have begun to show Your servant Your greatness and Your mighty hand, for what god is there in heaven or on earth who can do anything like Your works and Your mighty deeds?*
>
> *Deuteronomy 3:23-24 (NKJV)*

Believe it or not, God is mighty! We need to understand Him in this light. Understanding God in this manner starts from our thoughts; consequently our words and actions follow. We must dare His words.

To be victorious in God, we must be willing to obey and do His Word completely and totally. This is why we must know or identify our part of what to do, from His Word, which is the Bible or in our quiet time of prayer. If we are able to identify or know our part of "doing" and doing it obediently, correctly and consistently, to the end we will surely have the right result that will be evident to all. Everyone (except the blind) can see trees when they bear fruits. Sometimes, our "doing" may not give us the result that could be seen immediately. But **each time we do or obey the Word of God, like a tree, our root that is unseen is growing deeper and deeper until it reaches the stratum of soil with the nourishment that will convey our breakthrough or our desired expectation.** This is the root that gives us firmness and stability. It keeps us forever, against any storm of life; ensures nourishment in season and out of season like the palm planted by the rivers of waters; Psalm I: 3. It requires a process. It must start, continue and finish before any result can be achieved. Usually this process is challenged from the beginning to the end by the devil. Therefore we must watch, pray and be alert until we achieve our desired result. There is no resting time.

> *Jesus told them another parable: "The kingdom of heaven is like a man who sowed good seed in his field. But while everyone was sleeping, his enemy came and sowed weeds among the wheat, and went away.*

> Matthew 13:24-26

When a farmer sows, the work has only just begun. Weeding the farm, keeping off the birds, and rodents becomes part of a process that continues till harvest. Each farmer has to devise his own methods to achieve this, because only he knows the terrain better. Some have come up with what they call "scarecrow". This is a kind of human caricature designed to keep away birds.

> *Then birds of prey came down on the carcasses, but Abram drove them away.*

> Genesis 15:11

In addition to all these, he prays for the rains to come down on the crops. Sending down the rain is God's responsibility and doing the others is ours. When we hear or receive a Word from God, we must devise our own weeding process and create our own scarecrow or else we will have no harvest. As the farmer is doing his part, he is also waiting patiently for the time of harvest. Provided the farmer continues doing his part to the end and is patient, he is bound to receive harvest.

Impatience sometimes results out of ignorance, laziness or not wanting to do our part in full. Once the farmer is able to do his entire requirement, and knows the duration of his harvest, he waits patiently. For God's instruction that we hear and receive, there is a 'doing part' for us. We need to identify this 'doing part' and do them to the end. Then, God, who is faithful will perform and complete His part. **When we fail to do our part, or fail to complete the whole process and we expect God to do His part, we act like a thief.** This is the case with many of our demands and hence there is either a delay or no answers at all. God is no respecter of persons. The day we study or hear the word of God, accept, understand and believe is when the Word, which is the seed, becomes planted in our heart. Thereafter, we begin to nurture by brooding over it; watering and meditating on it; removing the weeds by rejecting any contrary thoughts and doubts that the enemy may wish to sow in our heart. This process continues until we get the result we seek. Only mature trees bear fruit. This is hard work!

> *The hard-working farmer should be the first to receive a share of the crops.*
>
> 2 Timothy 2:6

In our obedience we need to "work hard" at the Word of God for it to bear fruit for us. Generally speaking, **the Word of God can be likened to a large bunch of keys. It requires understanding to identify which key is capable of opening which door.** Otherwise we keep trying and trying until death knocks at our door. It is better to spend adequate time to search and identify the right key for the right door. The Word of God contains all the keys to life's problems. Nothing new will happen that has no solution in the Bible. The Word of God is powerful but it is not for people who want it in comfort from the very beginning. We cannot want comfort and power at the same time. We just cannot browse through the Bible or do a onetime micro-wave study and expect to enjoy the power from the word of God to do something miraculous for us or for others through us. We just cannot from the beginning open and quote the

Bible as prayer and expect something to happen. That is noise, empty cymbals. The Bible is God's Word and it is based on principles, which we must acquire, adopt, apply; and must under-go a set of processes. The Apostles "met daily" in homes and temples, breaking bread, studying the Word and in prayers. Miracles poured down afterwards; Acts 2: 42- 46.

Here on earth we have a set of divine laws, governed by principles, and "whosoever" understands and applies them enjoys the benefit they bring. For example no matter who we are, if we throw something up it must come down by gravitational force. If we sow nothing we reap nothing. We will reap whatever we sow. That is the law of seed time, and harvest time. If we do the right thing at the right time we reap the right result. If we do the right thing at the wrong time we receive the wrong result. These and many more are not dependent on whether we believed or not: or whether we prayed or not. They depend entirely on "knowing", "doing" and "timing". These laws can be clearly seen and understood from what God has created (Romans1: 20).

We shall discuss some of these laws and principles in the following chapters.

# A Time For Everything

All living things grow. Growth is a process. Every process takes time: There is always a beginning and end time; anything in between means an incomplete process. On this part of life everything happens within a time frame. Growth brings change. Change has signs, which are evident to all who see and know. Everything concerning God, the things He created and the ways He operates happen within a period of time and goes through a process. Nothing works outside time and process except there is a direct instruction from the creator to achieve His divine purpose or mission, called the supernatural or miracles- the accelerated manifestation of something by divine intervention based on word of knowledge and power of the Holy Ghost - Joshua stopped the sun from setting and altered time, Elijah stopped rain from falling, the birth of Jesus etc.

Process and time work hand in hand. They are essential elements in God's ways of operation in this part of existence. Until the fullness of time and process no positive result can be achieved here on earth. Therefore, time is one of the major elements to contend with on earth.

## TIME

*There is a season and time for everything: a season and time for every activity under heaven. As the Bible says:*

> *To every thing there is a season, and a time to every purpose under the heaven:*

> *A time to be born, and a time to die; a time to plant, and a time to pluck up that which is planted;*
>
> *A time to kill, and a time to heal; a time to break down, and a time to build up;*
>
> *A time to weep, and a time to laugh; a time to mourn, and a time to dance;*
>
> *A time to cast away stones, and a time to gather stones together; a time to embrace, and a time to refrain from embracing;*
>
> *A time to get, and a time to lose; a time to keep, and a time to cast away;*
>
> *A time to rend, and a time to sew; a time to keep silence, and a time to speak;*
>
> *A time to love, and a time to hate; a time of war, and a time of peace*
>
> *Ecclesiastes 3:1—8 (KJV)*

Where we have time, know that process is also involved. Time cannot exist without a process for any activity under heaven. A process takes time. Time and process bring change - whether good or bad - depending on the individual, components or elements that are involved. Where time and process are involved, know that patience must be worked out. Without patience we cannot enjoy the benefits of time and process.

> *But the fruit of the Spirit is love, joy, peace, patience, kindness, goodness, faithfulness, gentleness and self-control. Against such things there is no law.*
>
> Galatians 5:22-23

The fruit of the Spirit is not what we manifest instantly after being saved, neither is it operated by fasting and prayers alone. It requires time to develop the fruit of the Spirit to maturity, which means we must go through a process of training in principles; through willingness, discipline, self-control, godly determination and obedience. We must fan it into operation by training. Only mature trees bear fruits. Fruits are harvested in their season; seasons come in their time. The end of every fruit-bearing tree is to bear fruits when they are fully-grown and mature. At different times in the life of a tree it depicts different characteristics before maturity. At maturity, if it fails to bear fruits as expected something is seriously wrong.

Time and process have been put in place as universal laws. Whether we know it or not; whether we believe it or not; they are binding on us and we live and operate within them. They are powerful tools from creation. Understanding them will make achieving results here on earth much easier and will help to encourage us in our journey to developing patience and hope.

Consider the farmer. He knows the kind of crop to plant and at what season or time. He understands the processes he must undergo and the things he must do for a good harvest to be achieved. Knowing all these things, he waits patiently in hope without unnecessary worries. He does his part faithfully- getting the farm land, clearing it, planting, weeding, watering, chasing away birds, restricting pests, animals, and rodents, etc. In other words, he keeps watching, praying and waiting patiently in hope for the time of harvest. At the fullness of time the crop grows and brings forth fruit. God has spoken everything to happen at a particular time. If we miss the timing, we miss the result and will have to wait until the next season. At the right time, there is sufficient grace, power or anointing for the right result. Anything that happens outside the "right" time and against natural laws may be called a "miracle". And for this to happen we will require a direct instruction from God, the maker Himself.

> *Jesus saith unto her, Woman, what have I to do with thee? mine hour is not yet come.*
>
> *His mother saith unto the servants, Whatsoever he saith unto you, do it.*
>
> *And there were set there six water pots of stone, after the manner of the purifying of the Jews, containing two or three firkins apiece.*

*Jesus saith unto them, Fill the water pots with water. And they filled them up to the brim.*

*And he saith unto them, Draw out now, and bear unto the governor of the feast. And they bare it.*

*When the ruler of the feast had tasted the water that was made wine, and knew not whence it was: (but the servants which drew the water knew;) the governor of the feast called the bridegroom,*

*And saith unto him, Every man at the beginning doth set forth good wine; and when men have well drunk, then that which is worse: but thou hast kept the good wine until now.*

*This beginning of miracles did Jesus in Cana of Galilee, and manifested forth his glory; and his disciples believed on him.*

*John 2:4 -.11 (KJV)*

Jesus Christ made so much reference to "time". This was to emphasize its importance. The following Scriptures attest to some of such references: Matthew 8:29; 13: 30; 24: 43; Mark 1:15; 13:26; John 4: 21-23; 5:25; 12:31; 13:1.

*Then the Word of the LORD came to him: "Go at once to Zarephath of Sidon and stay there. I have commanded a widow in that place to supply you with food." So he went to Zarephath. When he came to the town gate, a widow was there gathering sticks. He called to her and asked, "Would you bring me a little water in a jar so I may have a drink?" As she was going to get it, he called, "And bring me, please, a piece of bread.*

*1 Kings 17:8-11*

"Go at once," God said to Elijah because He knew how long it would take Elijah to get to the gate of Zarephath and how long it would take the widow to gather her sticks, eat her last meal and die. If there was a delay the conducive environment or power for the miracle would have dissipated or gone.

Again look at the death of Lazarus. When the news came that he was sick, Jesus Christ waited until the right time before He went. There is a time for everything. At the right time, the process in its fullness will bear fruit. The cycle will have been completed.

Imagine, for a moment, the experience of a farmer; a faithful hard working farmer who did all that was required to be done, but for some reason at the time of harvest was not available, he was somewhere else. His harvest will:

> Rot away,
> Be eaten by birds, or
> Get stolen by thieves.

God did His part by giving the farmer seed, ensuring the rains fell and the crops germinated; but He will not do the harvesting for the farmer. The farmer must be there to harvest his crops or make the necessary plans for the crops to be harvested.

Most of us have been faithful and hard working; praying and fasting, yet having no results. We have been wondering if God answers prayers. Yes, He does answer prayers but at His time and when as a Father He knows we are ready. The question is, are we in the fullness of His time? Have we been available at the harvest time or have we been going round in circles? In every gathering of God's people, three major things happen: a time for blessings: a time for refreshment, and a time for rebuking. God has the prerogative and power to decide what happens at what time or can ensure or make all happen at the same time. If we know the accurate timing we can enjoy them. However, if we do not know or understand the timing we will achieve nothing and keep going around in circles. Whether we believe or not, if we are able to think of the right thing at the right time; able to hear the right thing at the right time; able to do the right thing at the right time; able to be at the right place at the right time, certainly and surely we will get the right result, whether we prayed or not. Prayers only tell us what to do, how to do and when to do. Prayer times, therefore is a time of getting instructions from God or a time to praise and worship Him. This is because at the fullness of His time, the processes required should have been completed for the result to manifest. Angels are not created to think but to carry out and obey instructions given to them by God (Ps 103:20). The devil cannot kill us if we resist him. He only attempts when we do not get or understand instructions or distort the information we get or, cause a delay so that we do not get to the right place at the right time, or do the right thing at the right time thereby causing delays, distractions, and frustration. In our frustration we may curse God and death may come.

Whatever we are asking God for has a time span. Like every seed it needs time to mature before it can bear fruits. Once we are not there (physically and in spirit) that season or time is past, we have to wait for the next season. By this, we may keep going in circles, until frustration sets in and we miss the mark of salvation –the Israelites almost missed it. As a fact only a few of those who left Egypt originally made it to the Promised land. Think of occasions when we wanted something from a friend or have been invited for an interview at an appointed time and we missed it because we were not on time. We were told, 'sorry, you cannot have it, because you were late'. We will have to wait for another time. On the other hand if we got there earlier we may have gotten what we wanted. Think also of occasions when we had to visit a friend's house to pay him a casual visit without invitation and we found him celebrating an event. We joined in the celebrations even when we were unaware of it and did not have an invitation. It could even be that some of the people invited did not come at the right time and we had to eat their portion of food although we were not in the original plan. This is the importance of proper timing.

If we are unsure or do not understand God's timing, whenever we are going for any Christian activities, be there early and stay to the end. This is what I call "playing safe". God decides what to do, how to do it and when to do it. He is God. For some of us lateness to godly activities or programs has robbed us of blessing and greatness. We do this casually and without apology because we think it does not matter and we owe nobody an apology. We console ourselves by saying, "God is Spirit and those who serve Him should do so in spirit". God Himself has put right timing and process in place for us to use so as to enjoy our lives here on earth. He does His work in time through a process! To understand this better, imagine having an appointment with a king or with a head of state. Would we go late? Certainly not! But if we do, what do we think would happen? Imagine what will happen when our appointment is with the One who enthroned and can dethrone us, the One who created us for His pleasure. We should aim at being at the right place at the right time and see what God will do for us. Avoid lateness in all of life's endeavours. There is a blessing for punctuality.

"There is a time for the hatching of eggs; a time for the lava; a time for the pupa; a time for the butterfly, and a time for the butterfly to fly".

All these happen in the mystery of time and process.

# *Process*

The word "process" from the Collins easy Learning English Study Dictionary could be defined as a series of connected operations deliberately undertaken to achieve a desired or particular objective.

It can also mean forward movement or progress. Anything that has to do with forward movement involves activities that are connected. We must therefore be able to identify the connected operations or activities and make deliberate efforts to go through them to the end. Stopping at any of the operations means not getting to the end of the process and so not getting the final result. For a butterfly to enjoy its fullness as a butterfly it must undergo and complete its processes from the egg-lava-pupa before finally becoming a butterfly; then it can fly. Every stage is unique and very important, and aborting any one of them means aborting the whole butterfly. This is also true in the obedience of the Word of God. Either we obey to the end and enjoy the benefits or obey part and lose all. Hence it is commonly said, 99.9% obedience is disobedience. Nine percent tithe is not tithe – it is stealing says the Lord! Mal 3:8. This is because we did not get to the end of the process. This means we will not get the benefit of obedience or of the tithe. Going through the processes of an activity requires determination, willful effort and patience. Remember, to understand God and how He does His things we have to understand nature. Look at the process the butterfly has to undergo before becoming a beautiful butterfly. From the cocoon it breaks into lava; from lava to the pupa stage and from here to the butterfly. Look at the egg and the process the mother hen must undergo before the eggs are hatched into chicks before the adult hen. Look at Elisha and the process he went through before following Elijah and getting the double portion. He burnt everything (his plough, oxen, harness etc) that would hinder him and followed to the end. He worked so hard to ensure that he saw Elijah at the point of his (Elijah's) departure. That was how he was able to inherit a double portion of Elijah's anointing. The things of God is like a treasure a man finds; we must look for it and do all that is required; selling everything, giving up everything to possess and sustain; Mat 13:44-46.

Let us consider the cost of Salvation. God left His heavenly throne and took up the nature of sinful man. He was crucified, shed His blood (His ordinance declares that without the shedding of blood there can be no atonement for sin), died, was buried, rose the third day and ascended to Heaven. Finally, let us honestly examine our lives and the processes we have undergone to get to where we are today or the processes we need to undergo to be where we would want to be or, to reach our desired goals. We cannot bridge any of the processes on our own.

I implore you to face it! Become determined to undergo all the processes to the end; let God be the one to exempt us at His will, if He finds the need in order to accomplish a particular purpose. Half-baked bread is not good for consumption. It is fit only to be thrown away. So it is with a life or a mission that has not gone through a complete process.

> *For which of you, intending to build a tower, sitteth not down first, and counteth the cost, whether he have sufficient to finish it?*
>
> *Lest haply, after he hath laid the foundation, and is not able to finish it, all that behold it begin to mock him,*
>
> *Saying, This man began to build, and was not able to finish.*
>
> *Or what king, going to make war against another king, sitteth not down first, and consulteth whether he be able with ten thousand to meet him that cometh against him with twenty thousand?*
>
> *Or else, while the other is yet a great way off, he*
>
> *sendeth an ambassage, and desireth conditions of peace.*

> *So likewise, whosoever he be of you that forsaketh not all*
> *that he hath, he cannot be my disciple.*
>
> *Luke 14:28-33 (KJV)*

Counting the cost, either to build or to go to war, means identifying all the requirements involved and being willing to do them to the end. We must make up our mind not to give up against all odds until the end when all the processes must have been completed, which can only happen at the fullness of time. The danger of giving up at any stage is losing all that we have done, and our efforts become a waste of energy and time. Nothing will be left and nothing can be salvaged. Imagine what would happen if a mother hen stops or abandons the process of the incubation of her eggs half way. All the eggs will rot and there would be no hatched chicks. Imagine if the full process of salvation were not complete; that half way our Lord and Saviour Jesus Christ changed His mind in the Garden of Gethsemane. How would the world be today?

Are you born again? If you are not, don't delay to confess your sins, forsake them and invite Jesus Christ into your heart (See Acts 2:38 — 39; I John 1:9). Make Him your Lord and Saviour. If you fail to do this, you might not be able to go to the next level - the level of power, blessing and greatness.

Are you born again and have identified the processes you must undergo? Then make up your mind to do them to the end against all odds? Remember that quitting at whatever stage would mean losing everything and salvaging nothing.

# What It Means To Be Born Again

Revelation brings power and power brings greatness. Greatness is getting revelation and acting on it to the end against all opposition — until the desired result is achieved. Greatness depends on completion of time and process in an activity. Great people do not quit. They stay to the end. They are anxious about the end of the matter and the end of the matter is always better than the beginning. Great people understand what Apostle Paul meant when he wrote:

> "We are hard pressed on every side, but not crushed; perplexed, but not in despair; persecuted, but not abandoned; struck down, but not destroyed."

2 Corinthians 4:8-9

They press on against the odds; they keep going ahead, waiting patiently in hope until the fullness of time and completion of the process to realize their vision or revelation. The three Hebrew children, Shadrach, Meshach and Abednego demonstrated this very clearly:

> Then Nebuchadnezzar in his rage and fury commanded to bring Shadrach, Meshach, and Abed-nego. Then they brought these men before the king.
>
> Nebuchadnezzar spake and said unto them, Is it true, O Shadrach, Meshach, and Abed-nego, do not ye serve my gods, nor worship the golden image which I have set up?
>
> Now if ye be ready that at what time ye hear the sound of the cornet, flute, harp, sackbut, psaltery, and dulcimer,

*and all kinds of music, ye fall down and worship the image which I have made; well: but if ye worship not, ye shall be cast the same hour into the midst of a burning fiery furnace; and who is that God that shall deliver you out of my hands?*

*Shadrach, Meshach, and Abed-nego, answered and said to the king, O Nebuchadnezzar, we are not careful to answer thee in this matter.*

*If it be so, our God whom we serve is able to deliver us from the burning fiery furnace, and he will deliver us out of thine hand, O king.*

*But if not, be it known unto thee, O king, that we will not serve thy gods, nor worship the golden image which thou hast set up.*

*Daniel 3:13-18. (KJV)*

Great people have incredible faith. And this makes them desire more direct revelations from God by themselves. Great people are determined people, people of strong will and character. They are people who have conquered fear; not afraid of death or dying because of God's word. They believe the Word of God against all odds.

Abraham also exhibited greatness as the book of Hebrews tells us (Hebrews 11:11-19); as did Simeon and Anna who spent time in the temple waiting for the birth of the Messiah (Luke 2:25-38).

They work for and with God and so have become dependable and conversant with God and His ways of doing things. They fear God than man. They are not intimidated by anything other than the Voice and Word of God. The heavens are opened over them and everything they do prospers. Great people run the race marked out for them, know their purpose (Luke 4:16-21;John 12:27; John18: 37) and at the end of which say 'I have ran the race well and it is finished'; John 19:20;Acts 22:21; 11 Timothy 4:7.

Being born-again connotes that we have been born before. Thus, like Nicodemus, we may ask: "Can we enter our mother's womb to be born the second time?" From Genesis 1:3, we read the story of creation.

To every other thing that was created God said "let there be" and it was. Then God said it was good. Everything looked good except that there was nothing created to look after or take care of the good things God had created. Then God said, *"Let us make man in our own image and in our own likeness"*; and God made or formed the man. He did not speak the man into existence, but rather took His time to make man since the man was to represent Him as god here on earth.

> *And God said, Let us make man in our image, after our likeness: and let them have dominion over the fish of the sea, and over the fowl of the air, and over the cattle, and over all the earth, and over every creeping thing that creepeth upon the earth.*

> *So God created man in his own image, in the image of God created he him; male and female created he them.*

> *And God blessed them, and God said unto them, Be fruitful, and multiply, and replenish the earth, and subdue it: and have dominion over the fish of the sea, and over the fowl of the air, and over every living thing that moveth upon the earth.*

> *And God said, Behold, I have given you every herb bearing seed, which is upon the face of all the earth, and every tree, in the which is the fruit of a tree yielding seed; to you it shall be for meat.*

> *And to every beast of the earth, and to every fowl of the air, and to everything that creepeth upon the earth, wherein there is life, I have given every green herb for meat: and it was so.*

> *And God saw everything that he had made, and, behold, it was very good. And the evening and the morning were the sixth day.*

> *Genesis 1:26-31*

> *These are the generations of the heavens and of the earth when they were created, in the day that the LORD God made the earth and the heavens,*
>
> *And every plant of the field before it was in the earth, and every herb of the field before it grew: for the LORD God had not caused it to rain upon the earth, and there was not a man to till the ground.*
>
> *But there went up a mist from the earth, and watered the whole face of the ground.*
>
> *And the LORD God formed man of the dust of the ground, and breathed into his nostrils the breath of life; and man became a living soul.*
>
> *Genesis 2:4-7 (KJV)*

The man was made from the dust of the earth and was not a living being until God breathed His own breath into the heap of dust. The breath of God represented His nature, His character, His powers, His essence and His life. This breath was composed of the Spirit of Life; Spirit of God consciousness; the Spirit of power and dominion; the Spirit of love; the Spirit of obedience: the Spirit of wisdom, and the Spirit of peace. With this, God equipped man for the assignment He gave him on earth; giving power and authority to him over the earth; giving him charge of the earth.

This same breath enabled man to have fellowship with God and 'act god' on earth. I call this divine breath the "battery of man", or 'the kingdom of the world'; without which man could not 'act god' on earth and could not be connected in any way with and to God (Psalm 82:6). This "could not" is what can be referred to as death. Death simply means the absence of God or 'no connection' with God. No torch can operate without energy; no vehicle can operate without an engine; no engine can operate without batteries. It simply becomes a carcass; beautiful on the outside, but hollow, functionless, and powerless inside or within.

The process by which this battery works can be likened to the solar energy cells, which obtain energy from the sun, and discharges energy during operations; and recharges by obtaining more sunlight. The longer such solar-powered batteries are deprived of sunlight, the less they perform, until they finally 'die'. As long as they have access to the sun they renew their energy. This was what God intended man to be. Whenever God visited the garden, man was recharged. This was to be a continuous process making the man to live forever. Man was not created to die or to be separated from God but to live forever for and with God, thus making man to be god here on earth.

With these characteristics of man, he was then made to reproduce his kind to fill the earth; to produce many gods that will represent God on the face of the earth, to always be able to discharge his duties and recharge when in contact with God. Man was therefore designed to live from everlasting to everlasting. He was to be an ambassador here on earth. He was to keep the fact in view that he was accountable to the Almighty God, his creator. The inability to function properly and recharge can also be termed death. When we do not have access to the re-charger, we die.

This glorious ambience, harmonious relationship, is what the Bible describes as "very good", Gen 1: 31. Subsequently every other thing God made was brought to the man to name; and whatever the man called it, it was. This relationship existed between God and man until man was deceived, and he handed over his "battery"; "the kingdom of the world", to angel Lucifer, who on account of his rebellion assumed the title "the devil". More of the devil's exposure is in my other book "The Victory Within". Soon after that happened man lost His charger through separation, that is death. The devil knowing what man had, turned everything to the opposite of what God had intended. The Spirit of Life gave way to the spirit of separation, which is death; the Spirit of God-consciousness was changed to become the spirit of self-consciousness. Man became more conscious of himself and his environment than of God who created him. Power went to the devil through this transaction and man became powerless. The spirit of love became the spirit of hate; the spirit of obedience became the spirit of disobedience; the spirit of peace turned to the spirit of war; wisdom became foolishness. The devil took advantage of the dominion and power now placed in his hands to manipulate man and man became extremely wicked; totally separated from God and allied to the devil rather than God. From this point the devil became the god of the earth and man became his slave; became powerless and lost the character and the nature of God.

In this condition man began to reproduce after his own kind rather than reproduce after God's kind. This was the genesis of the slave mentality, the tragedy that befell creation.

Through one man came separation from God or death. This is every man's state or position at birth.

Thus, every man is originally born in rebellion, sin, wickedness and powerlessness into a powerfully demonic world. We are born self-conscious rather than God-conscious; born in hatred rather than in love; born in disobedience; born into manipulations rather than doing things at appointed times and process; born separated from God and under the control of the devil. Flesh became powerful under the domain and control of the devil making man a slave, wholly manipulated by fear and the flesh. What makes people to take advantage of others is the quest for power and position. The devil having been given the power used it to also take his position. He now has an advantage and man became his laboratory for manipulations against man's choice, his will and against God. The first birth! Man fell under the flesh and its associated effect is sin. In order for God to progress in His plans He had to deal with the "sin" of man in the flesh, the Adamic 'sin'; John1: 29. Since God had already formed man and he had started reproducing after his kind, He had to come as a reproduced man in order to progress to the fullness of His plans. He came in the Person of Baby Jesus, but born by a virgin, to distinguish him from every man, thereby making it easy for anyone who is open minded to quickly recognize him; Mat 1:23. He came by the method He created; He underwent and grew through the processes (that He instituted) to manhood, learning self control, self discipline, God consciousness, use of power and dominion, love, obedience, wisdom and peace; teaching us how to conquer the flesh, showed us how to restore the character and nature of God that we lost. This He did through a set of Godly principles by the way He lived and taught; (Acts 1:1), and later took away the dominion and powers, from the devil;(Col 2:15), and giving it to anyone who believes; (John1:12). He became the substitute for our sins and reconciled those who believe back to God; (Rom 8:3).

Therefore, when man acknowledges this substitution work of Jesus Christ; says the sinner's prayer, forsakes his evil ways and invites Christ into his life as Lord and saviour he becomes born again: second birth, all his sins are forgiven and the power he lost is restored to him. That's why Jesus says:

> "*I have given you authority to trample on snakes and scorpions and to overcome all the power of the enemy; nothing will harm you. However, do not rejoice that the spirits submit to you, but rejoice that your names are written in heaven*".

> Luke 10:19-20

Being born-again places a man on a higher level than the devil, taking from the devil the powers, which gave him undue advantage over man. That is the power Adam and Eve gave to him. Being a Christian or Christ-like is not a religion. It is about a way of thinking and doing things; a way of using godly principles to demonstrate the character and the nature of God; bringing back the kingdom of God that existed in Eden before the fall; It's about taking dominion over the worldly fleshly nature making man one in character with God; Col 3:1-17 attest to a continuous godly character building, as a way of life for every Christian living.

> *The next day John saw Jesus coming toward him and said, Look, the Lamb of God, who takes away the SIN of the world! This is the one I meant when I said, 'A man who comes after me has surpassed me because he was before me.' I myself did not know him, but the reason I came baptizing with water was that he might be revealed to Israel.*" *Then John gave this testimony: "I saw the Spirit come down from heaven as a dove and remain on him. I would not have known him, except that the one who sent me to baptize with water told me, 'The man on whom you see the Spirit come down and remain is he who will*

*baptize with the Holy Spirit.' I have seen and I testify that this is the Son of God.*

John 1:29-34

*And having disarmed the powers and authorities, he made a public spectacle of them, triumphing over them by the cross.*

Colossians 2:15

The things about God progresses and grows; everything God has created continues. It is never the same. For this reason, God did not have to create another man when the first man fell, because the power to reproduce had been activated in the man. God continued by using the process He has given the man to reproduce to manifest Himself. This He did in the Baby Jesus. This is progress. It is like a student who fails his exams and has to repeat the class. Though the student failed, yet some progress has been made, because the student is not exactly the same as when he first got into the class. He has made some progress in knowledge, no matter how little. He has learnt something to make him different from the new entrants that will come to join him in that class.

Being born again is realizing what Adam and Eve had done by removing man from alignment in God. This made us available to the devil, separating us from God, thereby inhibiting us from recharging our "batteries". We became dead spiritually. Being born- again is realizing our fallen state, moving away from our loss of dominion, power, authority on earth; lack of God consciousness, love, obedience, wisdom peace; inability to function properly to recharge, to appreciating God by connecting back to Him and experiencing the love of God; His grace and redemption through His Son Jesus Christ, all at His own expense.

*HOW CAN THIS BE? SHALL WE ENTER OUR MOTHERS WOMB A SECOND TIME?*

No. Flesh gives birth to flesh and spirit gives birth to spirit. The things of the spirit are perceived and received by faith. It is impossible to please God without faith (Hebrews 11:6). *Man fell in the Garden of Eden, because of lack of faith and trust in God.* Man has been tormented by his fall because of his seeing- before-believing syndrome. The fall has made man to look more to other men first for the things of God rather than looking unto God his Creator.

> *But the people refused to listen to Samuel. "No!" they said. "We want a king over us. Then we will be like all the other nations, with a king to lead us and to go out before us and fight our battles."*

Samuel 8:19-20

God wanted man to take Him at His Word by faith and believe Him for who He is. Man wanted to see, touch and feel before believing. God - our Father - in His love, descended until He could descend no further by becoming man, John 1:14. He descended to the very bottom, which is hell to set people free by taking the dominion and power which the devil had been using to manipulate man. How great is His love! Before man fell, God did not require any sacrifices or offering from him. He only wanted a relationship, which would enable His children to represent Him as god here on earth. He wanted communion; He wanted true friendship based on faith and love. He wanted nothing more and nothing less. He wanted man to worship Him in spirit and in truth. He wanted everything that He had created to live and work in harmony, so He brought them to the man to name. When He saw how man participated in creation by naming the creatures, and working in love and harmony; He said it was good. Then He rested, being assured the man was in charge.

God Himself did the first animal sacrifice after the man fell. This sacrifice had a two-fold purpose: to cleanse man with blood and to cover his nakedness with the skin of the animal. This was where God instituted the process of cleansing of sins by animal blood, which was later replaced by the Blood of Christ as final atonement.

> *God made garments of skin for Adam and his wife and clothed them. And the LORD God said, "The man has become one of us to know good and evil. And now must not be allowed to reach out his hand and take also from*

57

*the tree of life and eat, and live forever." So the LORD God banished him from the Garden of Eden to work the ground from which he had been taken. After he drove the man out, he placed on the east side of the Garden of Eden cherubim and a flaming sword flashing back and forth to guard the way to the tree of life.*

Genesis 3: 21-24

Being born-again could be likened to making a return to the Garden of Eden before the fall. It is the creation of a new kingdom ruled by God. It is the removing of the banishment that was placed by God. It has to do with godly relationships and the development of godly nature and character that we lost in Eden, which was His original intention for creating man. We need to understand how all this concept of being born-again started and culminated into our Lord and Saviour Jesus Christ: the final mediator between man and God, the only way to God and the Light of the world. In His light we see light. He is also called the last Adam. This denotes that there was a first Adam and emphatically means there will be no other after Jesus Christ, the second and last Adam. Everything started with Him and everything will end with Him.

God is God. We better believe it. No man can decode Him and that is why He is God. We either believe or take Him for who He is or not. He has made all this clear so that we should not stress ourselves much but to simply believe, trust and obey. However, He has revealed to us what He wants us to know and sometimes depending on our personal relationship and obedience to Him, He might reveal more things to us about others, His plans or about ourselves. Our intimacy with Him determines how far He directs us. As the Bible says:

*The secret things belong to the LORD our God, but the things revealed belong to us and to our children forever, that we may follow all the words of this law.*

Deuteronomy 29:29

We should ensure we work by what we know, have clearly understood and believed. What we may not understand, we should work or walk or believe by faith in His Word, His priests, or ask God through prayers and fasting. This is why faith is an essential element. Faith is the foundation, or beginning point of our belief. Blessed are those who do not see or understand and yet believe.

> *And I say unto you, Ask, and it shall be given you; seek, and ye shall find; knock, and it shall be opened unto you.*
>
> *For every one that asketh receiveth; and he that seeketh findeth; and to him that knocketh it shall be opened.*
>
> *If a son shall ask bread of any of you that is a father, will he give him a stone? or if he ask a fish, will he for a fish give him a serpent?*
>
> *Or if he shall ask an egg, will he offer him a scorpion?*
>
> *If ye then, being evil, know how to give good gifts unto your children: how much more shall your heavenly Father give the Holy Spirit to them that ask him?*
>
> Luke 11:9-13 (KJV)

In our walk of faith with God we must come to the point where we believe Him for ourselves and not only because of what other people may tell us or do. This is the point where faith, which cannot be tossed about by any form of doctrine or uprooted by the storms of life, takes root. We must learn to seek God for ourselves and by ourselves in the major issues of life. God is for everyone. He is not the exclusive right of any particular person. He reveals things and Himself to "whosoever wills". He is a fair, righteous and just God and Father. We are His children. Before the era of being born again, God only revealed Himself to one person at a time:

> *And God said, "I will be with you. And this will be the sign to you that it is I who have sent you: When you have brought the people out of Egypt, you will worship God on this mountain".*
>
> Exodus 3:12

God is spirit and can work in and through us. All our enquiry about God, confessions to God, instructions on restitution, etc., came from God by His Spirit to people through the man He chose to use. The Jews of old had all sorts of names for these people: Priests, Levites, Prophets, etc., who enquired on behalf of the people for God from within an enclosure in the temple of God called the Holy of Holies; the "most inner" court, where the Ark of God was. The Ark denotes the habitation of God. It was the exclusive right of the High Priest to enter the Holy of Holies for the people, once a year.

> *The priest who is anointed and ordained to succeed his father as high priest is to make atonement. He is to put on the sacred linen garments and make atonement for the Most Holy Place, for the Tent of Meeting and the altar, and for the priests and all the people of the community. "This is to be a lasting ordinance for you: Atonement is to be made once a year for all the sins of the Israelites." And it was done, as the LORD commanded Moses.*

> Leviticus 16:32-34

We are insatiable; difficult to please, but God was trying to please us without force because of His love. He wanted to do it by making our hearts willing. The people of Israel of old kept grumbling and complaining about their leaders and God kept making it easier for them to be able to follow and obey Him. Sometimes they complained and displayed great unbelief.

> *Miriam and Aaron began to talk against Moses because of his Cushite wife, for he had married a Cushite. "Has the LORD spoken only through Moses?" they asked. "Hasn't he also spoken through us?" And the LORD heard this.*

> Numbers 12:1-2

In Numbers 16:1-3, we read about the rebellion of Korah, Abiram and Dathan:

> *'Korah son of Izhar, the son of Kohath, the son of Levi, and certain Reubenites — Dathan and Abiram, Sons of Eliab, and On son of Peleth — became insolent and rose up against Moses. With them were 250 Israelite men, well-known community leaders who had been appointed members of the council. They came as a group to oppose Moses and Aaron and said to them, "You have gone too far! The whole community is holy; every one of them and the LORD is with them. Why then do you set yourselves above the LORD's assembly?"*

Man began to hunger and thirst for direct personal contact with God. They wanted laws directly from God and not from any intermediary. God in answer to that gave us the Ten Commandments and the Laws. One of such laws is that sin cannot be forgiven without blood, as Hebrews 9:22 tells us:

> *In fact, the law requires that nearly everything be cleansed with blood and without the shedding of blood there is no forgiveness."*

People live in sin daily and without cleansing by the blood we can never approach God in any form. Before Jesus Christ came the law required people to be cleansed using the blood of animals, bulls, lamb, goats, pigeons, etc.

# Animal Sacrifice

In Leviticus 4:1-12 (KJV) we read:

*And the LORD spake unto Moses, saying,*

*Speak unto the children of Israel, saying, If a soul shall sin through ignorance against any of the commandments of the LORD concerning things which ought not to be done, and shall do against any of them:*

*If the priest that is anointed do sin according to the sin of the people; then let him bring for his sin, which he hath sinned, a young bullock without blemish unto the LORD for a sin offering.*

*And he shall bring the bullock unto the door of the tabernacle of the congregation before the LORD; and shall lay his hand upon the bullock's head, and kill the bullock before the LORD.*

*And the priest that is anointed shall take of the bullock's blood, and bring it to the tabernacle of the congregation:*

*And the priest shall dip his finger in the blood, and sprinkle of the blood seven times before the LORD, before the vail of the sanctuary.*

*And the priest shall put some of the blood upon the horns of the altar of sweet incense before the LORD, which is in the tabernacle of the congregation: and shall pour all the blood of the bullock at the bottom of the altar of the burnt offering, which is at the door of the tabernacle of the congregation.*

*And he shall take off from it all the fat of the bullock for the sin offering; the fat that covereth the inwards, and all the fat that is upon the inwards,*

*And the two kidneys, and the fat that is upon them, which is by the flanks, and the caul above the liver, with the kidneys, it shall he take away,*

*As it was taken off from the bullock of the sacrifice of peace offerings: and the priest shall burn them upon the altar of the burnt offering.*

*And the skin of the bullock, and all his flesh, with his head, and with his legs, and his inwards, and his dung,*

*Even the whole bullock shall he carry forth without the camp unto a clean place, where the ashes are poured out, and burn him on the wood with fire: where the ashes are poured out shall he be burnt.*

The type of sin would determine the kind of animal sacrifice and he would take the prescribed animal to the priest to perform the necessary requirements of the law, according to instructions. But man's insatiability and fastidiousness continued. When people sinned, the requirement from God through the priest for atonement would be made known and may be a bull but where the sinner could not afford a bull, negotiations continued to sometimes the least, to say a pigeon. Where the person could not afford a pigeon, this may lead to the person's death. This posed a problem, thereby increasing grumbling, complaining. Meanwhile God, as a Father, is compassionate and loving to forgive. Yet He cannot do it without the blood. The blood signifies death, because the life of an animal is in the blood. People are not on equal basis and sins have different magnitudes. All the requirements for atonement for sin needed to be made equal, because Priests may not hear correctly, or their emotions may becloud their sense of judgment especially when it is about matters concerning loved ones. Sometimes they did not know where to draw the line because of the flesh. Priests are humans! Being born again reconciles and restores man's relationship with God thereby placing him where he should be; removing every form of excuse except the one that is self-imposed, which is self-deception. How we progress with God and in our relationship with Him is now a choice that we can determine for ourselves.

Man is a tool in the hand of God. Man is the dwelling temple of God. Therefore it is the Spirit of God in man that makes man to express the goodness of God to man. What makes a man is the spirit that is in the man, not his outward appearance, which is the flesh. It is the spirit in us that make us who we are. It is our attitude or character or action that determines who is operating or working in us: either the devil or God. This means our earth body can either be the house from which God operates or the temple from which the devil operates. This will depend on the door we open and who we permit to come in. If the wrong door is opened wrong things will get into the house; Matthew 16: 17, 23; Luke 22:3; John 13:27.

The real man is our spirit, which manifests outwardly for people to see. This was what the Lord Jesus Christ was trying to explain that God could live in any man who opens his heart to Him. This is why He chose to manifest Himself through the Priests, Levites, the Prophets, etc., but man did not understand. He came Himself as Jesus Christ to make known this fact, yet the religious leaders of that age, including His disciples, still failed to understand.

> *In John 14:8-11, we read that Philip said, "Lord, show us the Father and that will be enough for us." Jesus answered: "Don't you know me, Philip, even after I have been among you such a long time? Anyone who has seen me has seen the Father. How can you say, 'Show us the Father'? Don't you believe that I am in the Father, and that the Father is in me? The words I say to you are not just my own. Rather, it is the Father, living in me, who is doing his work. Believe me when I say that I am in the Father and the Father is in me; or at least believe on the evidence of the miracles themselves".*

The miracles; great wonders, good works men have performed, were not done by them but God working in and through them. Being born again is substituting our body for the Ark of God or becoming His temple for Him to live in, and work through to establish His kingdom on earth. The Holy of Holies was the exclusive right of the High Priest who took the blood of animals there to atone for his sins first before that of the people, and to enquire from God. This place was hidden from all. It was never open or exposed; it was the place where the Ark of God (our bodies when we become born again) was kept; representing the secret dwelling of the Most High God. This place had no grace. The moment the high priest enters with any sin he dies. Hence the priest of old would tie rope with bells around their waist and be in constant motion for people in the middle court to hear the dangling. The rope extended to the middle court, so that when the ringing of the bells ceased, it meant that the priest was dead; and the people in the middle court would pull his corpse out with the rope. This place was not an ordinary place, but being born again now gives one access to the Holy of Holies. It is now open to all who are born again to enter freely. The Holy of Holies is now in the heart of every believer, because he has become the temple of God by His Holy Spirit; Hebrews chapters 8, 9 and 10.

God came in human form, in flesh and blood, because man fell under flesh and blood. God substituted Himself for the sin sacrifices of lamb, bull, goat, pigeon, etc. He died to shed His blood ONCE AND FOR ALL (John 1: 29). Thus, all who believe and confess their sins are forgiven and are born again.

> *It was now about the sixth hour, and darkness came over the whole land until the ninth hour, for the sun stopped shining. And the curtain of the temple was torn in two. Jesus called out with a loud voice, "Father, into your hands I commit my spirit." When he had said this, he breathed his last. The centurion, seeing what had happened, praised God and said, "Surely this was a righteous man." When all the people who had gathered to witness this sight saw what took place, they beat their breasts and went away. But all those who knew him,*

*including the women who had followed him from Galilee,*
*stood at a distance, watching these things.*

Luke 23:44-49

This, among many other distinguishing facts, made Jesus Christ different from all who came before Him. He is the Son of God. He is the first from among the dead. He is the living Redeemer. He is the only mediator between man and God. He is the Saviour of the world, the Lamb of God who takes away the sin of the world. He is the horn of our salvation; the wonderful way-maker; our soon coming King of kings, and Lord of lords. He is the last Adam and He is our Righteousness in God.

As the Bible says in Romans 10:8-13: '*...the word is near you; it is in your mouth and in your heart, that is, the word of faith we are proclaiming: That if you confess with your mouth, "Jesus is Lord," and believe in your heart that God raised him from the dead, you will be saved. For it is with your heart that you believe and are justified, and it is with your mouth that you confess and are saved. As the Scripture says, "Anyone who trusts in him will never be put to shame." For there is no difference between Jew and Gentile-the same Lord is Lord of all and richly blesses all who call on him, for, Everyone who calls on the name of the Lord will be saved*'.

We do not require any bull or lamb; we do not require any goat or pigeons; we do not require even water to cleanse our soul because it cannot. We do not need to travel to Jerusalem or anywhere. All we need is our mouth to confess our sins and our heart to believe that through the blood of Jesus Christ, we have been forgiven and so we are saved. This is what it means to be born again. Men have become equal, in terms of the requirement for the forgiveness of sins, in the sight of God. Now man has no excuse to continue to live or remain in sin or 'death'. God has opened the door to His throne room of grace and given all men the right to enter and enjoy His free gift.

*For God so loved the world, that he gave his only begotten*
*Son, that whosoever believeth in him should not perish,*
*but have everlasting life.*

*For God sent not his Son into the world to condemn the world; but that the world through him might be saved.*

*He that believeth on him is not condemned: but he that believeth not is condemned already, because he hath not believed in the name of the only begotten Son of God.*

*And this is the condemnation, that light is come into the world, and men loved darkness rather than light, because their deeds were evil.*

*For every one that doeth evil hateth the light, neither cometh to the light, lest his deeds should be reproved.*

*But he that doeth truth cometh to the light, that his deeds may be made manifest, that they are wrought in God.*

*John 3:16-21 (KJV)*

There are no more excuses whether here on earth or above in heaven as Romans 1:18-20 tells us: '*...the wrath of God is being revealed from heaven against all the godlessness and wickedness of men who suppress the truth by their wickedness, since what may be known about God is plain to them, because God has made it plain to them. For since the creation of the world God's invisible qualities-his eternal power and divine nature-have been clearly seen, being understood from what has been made, so that men are without excuse*'.

To be born again means to believe, to receive the gift of grace, faith and forgiveness. Being born again has to do with having access to God without shame or reproach. It means that we can now return to the Garden of Eden, living, "naked and not ashamed." To be born again is not about religion or doctrine or defending God by forcing or killing others. It is about having a personal relationship with God, which must be developed and sustained. It means being conscious of the assignment He has for us after our redemption. It is about being part of the new coming kingdom, a people of Godly nature and character; a royal priesthood; a holy people.

In Matthew 28:19-20 *Jesus says, '...therefore go and make disciples of all nations, baptizing them in the name of the Father and of the Son and of* the Holy Spirit, and teaching them to obey everything I have commanded you. And surely I am with you always, to the very end of the age'.

When we become born again, we become the light of the world and the salt of the earth (Matthew 5:13-14).

Jesus once declared, "If I had not come and spoken to them, they would not be guilty of sin. Now, however, they have no excuse for their sin". (John 15:22).

*John 3:17-21 (KJV) also tells us:*

*'For God sent not his Son into the world to condemn the world; but that the world through him might be saved.*

*He that believeth on him is not condemned: but he that believeth not is condemned already, because he hath not believed in the name of the only begotten Son of God.*

*And this is the condemnation, that light is come into the world, and men loved darkness rather than light, because their deeds were evil.*

*For every one that doeth evil hateth the light, neither cometh to the light, lest his deeds should be reproved.*

*But he that doeth truth cometh to the light, that his deeds may be made manifest, that they are wrought in God.*

# The Open Door

The Bible says in Revelations 3:7:

*To the angel of the church in Philadelphia write:*

*These are the words of him who is holy and true, who holds the key of David. What he opens no one can shut, and what he shuts no one can open. I know your deeds. See, I have placed before you an open door that no one can shut.*

The door is open and no one can shut it except us. A man can shut the door against himself through fear of persecution or the quest to please man rather than God. Self-deception, plain refusal to live by the truth which has been made known from ages past, unbelief, hardness of heart, and failure to seek God are other causes where we can shut the door against ourselves.

Each positive step is advancement. When we get saved we all start with a clean slate with God. Thus we all have the same starting point, but how far we go or can go will depend largely on us, individually. Every development of God must start little by little because each little process has an experience to be learnt which will aid the next one. Several Scriptures illustrate this point:

*Do not be terrified by them, for the LORD your God, who is among you, is a great and awesome God. The LORD your God will drive out those nations before you, little*

> *by little. You will not be allowed to eliminate them all at once, or the wild animals will multiply around you".*

Deuteronomy 7:21-22

In Proverbs 13:11, we read; *"Dishonest money dwindles away, but he who gathers money little by little makes it grow".*

On this side of life living things grow. Growth starts little by little through processes and principles. It has a beginning and an end. It has the premature stage and the mature stage. Different things attract different stages and each stage has its characteristics and requirements. Skipping any stage will delay the training requirement for the next stage or the whole process can be aborted. Any man who attempts to grow big at once will not only be miserable, but might end up not making it at all. It is easier for those who think "sudden greatness" or "riches" to easily alienate themselves from the things or ways and will of God than those who learn to go along little by little. Hence the Bible says you should not think of yourself more highly than you ought:

> *"For by the grace given me I say to every one of you: Do not think of yourself more highly than you ought, but rather think of yourself with sober judgment, in accordance with the measure of faith God has given you."*

Romans 12:3-4

If we have not believed God for a bicycle, it will be foolhardy to begin to believe Him for an airplane. Faith must grow. Whether born in the physical or in the spirit, we must start as a baby. Babies must grow to maturity before they can reproduce or be able to enjoy certain goodly benefits. Certain benefits are for matured people while some are for infants:

> *Like newborn babies, crave pure spiritual milk, so that by it you may grow up in your salvation, now that you have tasted that the Lord is good.*

1 Peter 2:2-3

*In fact, though by this time you ought to be teachers,
you need someone to teach you the elementary truths of
God's word all over again. You need milk, not solid food!
Anyone who lives on milk, being still an infant, is not
acquainted with the teaching about righteousness. But
solid food is for the mature, who by constant use have
trained themselves to distinguish good from evil.*

Hebrews 5:12-14

All babies, whether physical or spiritual, need food to grow. As we grow from infancy to maturity, we begin to reproduce

*All flesh is not the same: Men have one kind of flesh;
animals have another, birds another and fish another.
There are also heavenly bodies and there are earthly
bodies; but the splendour of the heavenly bodies is one
kind, and the spender of the earthly bodies is another.
The sun has one kind of splendour, the moon another and
the stars another; and star differs from star in splendour.*

Corinthians 15:3941

In the same way that all flesh are not the same so it is that the processes and time of maturity are not the same; neither are their methods of bearing fruits the same. They are unique in their own ways. A tomato seed and a mango seed do not have the same time of germination, growth and maturity. They are all different. A butterfly does not become a beautiful butterfly in just one day. It starts from being an egg; then develops to lava; then a caterpillar, and finally a butterfly. It goes through process and time. If for any reason it failed to complete or go through any of the processes it will never become a butterfly. If it attempts to short-circuit time and process, it would either die prematurely or suffer some deformity. In this incomplete process, it might either be food for its predators or will not be able to perform all the functions of a butterfly. It may never enjoy all the privileges and rights of a butterfly. It becomes unfit as a butterfly. All living things created by God develop and grow including the things of the spirit.

Nothing living remains static. There is a beginning and there is an end. The variables are time and process. With regards to the things of the spirit our willingness, patience, and determination are the parameters for process. It is the end that determines the result.

> *"The end of a matter is better than its beginning, and patience is better than pride."*

Ecclesiastes 7:8

Once we are born again, a door of adoption as a son is opened by God. We either stare at it, thus remain a baby; or we walk through it to fullness by growing into maturity. This is a choice we must make.

Prophet Moses saw the Promised Land but did not enter. We can see and not enter. We can be born again and not enjoy all the benefits. What we do with what we see is very important and this is what makes the difference between people. Adam and Eve saw the fruit and ate in disobedience. They brought death to the entire human race. King David saw Beersheba and slept with her, bringing curses upon his entire family, Jesus Christ was shown and in fact offered the kingdoms of the world with the promise to be given it only if He would bow to and worship the devil; but Jesus resisted the offer by reminding the devil that God alone deserves our worship. What we do with what we are reading today is the same as what we are seeing. What we do and how we react will make a difference in our life. (Matthew 18:3).

In 2004, an Ex-President of the Federal Republic of Nigeria, while on a working visit to Akwa Ibom State, opened the door of adoption into his family to a young boy whose parents were not well to do, like him. The door was opened, but the choice to enter or not was solely the boy's. God has thrown wide open His door of adoption to us. We are the ones to choose to walk in, walk through, walk away or shut it against ourselves forever.

# The Secret Spirit

The things of the spirit start from servanthood. As soon as man sinned in the Garden of Eden he became a slave-servant to the devil. Man no longer had any choice of his own. His life, liberty, and property were under the absolute control of Satan. Man became mentally subjected to Lucifer's whims and desires, his ways, vices and influences; all contrary to God's original purpose and plans.

Man became extremely evil and wicked. This grieved God, prompting His desire to wipe out the entire human race and every other living species (Genesis 6:5-7); Grace kept and saved Noah and his family.

All the many points that have been discussed in this book culminate in the knowledge that leads to the path of 'The Secret Verse' - learning and growing into maturity to be able to manifest as sons and daughters of God. This is the secret kept hidden for many years, which Jesus Christ came to reveal. It is subtle, quiet, gentle and yet powerful to those who understand it. Consider these Words of Jesus:

> "I no longer call you servants, because a servant does not know his master's business. Instead, I have called you friends, for everything that I learned from my Father I have made known to you".

> John 15:15

We have slave-servants (different from born- servants, i.e. those who willingly serve or want to serve) mentality before we turn to God through Jesus Christ. This is the "seed" or starting point. When we turn to God, we are saying 'Jesus, take us to your home, or to your family, I want to serve you so as to get close to your family. Transform me from the kingdom of darkness, slave mentality to the family of the beloved. Help turn my thinking to become your friend. The Bible says:

> *When the two disciples heard him say this, they followed Jesus. Turning around, Jesus saw them following and asked, "What do you want?" They said, "Rabbi" (which means Teacher), "where are you staying?""Come," he replied, "and you will see." So they went and saw where he was staying, and spent that day with him. It was about the tenth hour.*

John 1:37-39

The slave-Servant mentality is what should first be broken when we become born again. It is the commencement process for adoption as a son or daughter of God. This was the seed sown in our hearts when we lived in sin after the fall of man. This is the humbling stage; the stage we submit ourselves to authority: a time we cast down our crown, title and serve, against all odds. If we cannot develop the habit of a humble servant, our seed dies. This occurs through pride, arrogance, and self-exaltation. When we pass the humbling test then we will be exalted. Everyone would want to be a servant in the palace of the king to get to the king; associate with the palace in hope for other benefits. How wonderful to be a servant in the kingdom of God to get close to God and enjoy many endless benefits. A servant is a whole man except for his thinking and his ways of doing things. As a man thinks in his heart so is he. Our thinking has great influence in our actions and the way we do things.

> *For as he thinks in his heart, so is he.*

Proverbs 23:7a (NKJV)

The following are some characteristics or mentality of a slave-servant thinking pattern:

He is employed to do a particular kind of job or work.

He does not go outside what he was paid to do.

He does not go the extra mile without asking for the extra cost.

He does not give in to extra time. Once his engaged time is up he stops work.

He plays truancy when the master is away.

He is always looking for the least opportunity to cheat or to lie because he wants more than he has actually worked for.

He hardly ever thinks that where he is working can one day belong to him.

He feels inferior to the children of the owner.

He has no mind of his own.

He hardly can take a decision, let alone take a risk, in regard to the employer for fear of making a mistake that can lead to a sack or punishment.

He is always afraid of getting sacked.

He is always complaining and grumbling.

He does not know much about his master's business.

He limits himself in regard to freedom in the master's affairs. There are many no go areas in his mind.

He deserts his master when the master is unable to pay him his wages.

He has no deep relationship with his master other than his wages that are due him.

He cannot inherit the master's business.

How successful we work and live over the above mentality will determine greatly when the master will say, "I no longer call you servant but friend".

# The Spirit Of A Friend

Friendship is a higher relationship than that of a slave-servant. The way a friend does things is different from that of a slave-servant. A friend goes the extra mile having caught the mission and vision of his master. A friend has come to understand his master and has developed more intimacy and trust in his master. A friend does not work just for his wages. He looks and works for the success of the venture. He stands in the gap between his master and the success of the venture. He has become willing to make sacrifices. Little wonder Jesus says:

> "Greater love has no one than this that he lay down his life for his friends. You are my friends if you do what I command".

> John 15:13-14

Obedience flows naturally between friends and they relate easier and freer, because they are allies. Friends don't pass instructions from one to the other like in the slave-servant and master relationship, but discuss freely and face-to-face with one another.

> The LORD would speak to Moses face to face, as a man speaks with his friend.

> Exodus 33:11

The atmosphere becomes friendlier rather than the tense atmosphere of the master - servant relationship.

The relationship has grown from being a servant to that of a friend. The master is friendlier. At this point we are servants by choice.

# The Spirit Of A Brother

Friends, like slave-servants also have limitations in their way of doing and thinking. There is an extent a friend can accomplish in a business. Thus, to climb into a richer relationship, the realm of friendship must diminish and die to another stage. This is the stage of becoming a brother. This is another level of relationship in which our thinking will have to be affected. Our commitments and responsibilities need to go beyond that of just being a friend. Unless there is a change, a friend can never think or do things as a brother. The degree of trust, loyalty and hope increases from just being a friend to a brother and the master has a greater hope that the venture can at least go beyond him. The openness becomes more. It is not now about remunerations but continuity. At least the master has the hope that the business would remain in the family. "Blood is thicker than water", they say, therefore the degree of sacrifice is much more than that of just a friend:

> "A friend loves at all times, and a brother is born for adversity".

> Proverbs 17:17

The way of thinking of a brother is determined by his desire to ensure success of the family business.

Brothers are willing to do what needs to be done to maintain the family name. The measure of a brother is in times of adversity. He stays longer than a friend as his stake is much more. Peter stayed with and followed Jesus Christ longer during his trial than the rest of the disciples. This was because Peter had the spirit of a brother. John 13:37 says, "...

Peter asked, "Lord, why can't I follow you now? I will lay down my life for you."

At this juncture only Peter depicted the characteristics of the spirit of brotherhood. No wonder Jesus Christ said to Peter "*...thou art Peter, and upon this rock I will build my church; and the gates of hell shall not prevail against it. And I will give unto thee the keys of the kingdom of heaven...*"; *Mat16: 18-19* KJV. After Jesus' resurrection, the others began to follow.

As Jesus said to Mary:

> "*Do not hold on to me, for I have not yet returned to the Father. Go instead to my brothers and tell them, 'I am returning to my Father and your Father, to my God and your God*"
>
> John 20:17

At this point the master begins to see the person as being born of the same parent, the degree of intimacy increases. Blood comes into the equation and strengthens the family relationship. The person begins to integrate as a family member. Major family responsibilities can now be entrusted. This was the case of Abraham and his servant:

> *And Abraham was old, and well stricken in age: and the LORD had blessed Abraham in all things.*
>
> *And Abraham said unto his eldest servant of his house, that ruled over all that he had, Put, I pray thee, thy hand under my thigh:*
>
> *And I will make thee swear by the LORD, the God of heaven, and the God of the earth, that thou shalt not take a wife unto my son of the daughters of the Canaanites,*
>
> *among whom I dwell:*
>
> *But thou shalt go unto my country, and to my kindred, and take a wife unto my son Isaac.*

*And the servant said unto him, Peradventure the woman will not be willing to follow me unto this land: must I needs bring thy son again unto the land from whence thou camest?*

*And Abraham said unto him, Beware thou that thou bring not my son thither again.*

*The LORD God of heaven, which took me from my father's house, and from the land of my kindred, and which spake unto me, and that sware unto me, saying, Unto thy seed will I give this land; he shall send his angel before thee, and thou shalt take a wife unto my son from thence.*

*And if the woman will not be willing to follow thee, then thou shalt be clear from this my oath: only bring not my son thither again.*

*And the servant put his hand under the thigh of Abraham his master, and sware to him concerning that matter.*

*Genesis 24:1-9 (KJV)*

This servant, after many years of service, obedience and faithfulness to Abraham had grown from a slave- servant to a friend, and finally to becoming a brother; one that could be trusted and depended upon to carry out the responsibility of picking a wife for Abraham's son, Isaac. A mere slave-servant or friend cannot carry out this major family responsibility of getting or marrying a wife for the one that is to become heir to the promise. It has to be a relationship that is more intimate. This is the brother stage. This stage should become much more intimate to those who believe in the Blood of Jesus Christ; the Blood that was shed on the cross of Calvary; the unifying Blood. Born again believers on account of this should do enduring prosperous businesses for generations to see and inherit.

# The Spirit Of A Son

*"Beware of your friends; do not trust your brothers. For every brother is a deceiver, and every friend a slanderer".*

Jeremiah 9:4

No matter the intimacy between a master and a brother, there is still a shaky hope in the mind of the master, because a brother can change when the master is no more. The venture can be taken away from the direct family of the master to that of the brothers. They can change the venture to belong to "themselves" thereby sending the master's name into oblivion. There are certain sacrifices a brother will not agree to make on behalf of another brother, especially when the master is no longer alive. Therefore there is limit to how far a brother can go. He may be freer and more trustworthy in the estimation of the master and his business. He may be loyal and committed. He may behave like he would die for the venture, like Apostle Peter. Still, whenever a master intends to hand over a venture to a brother he does it half -heartedly, because his hope is not sure, solid or properly anchored. He sees it as a bleak arrangement and grumbles within himself.

> *But Abram said, "Sovereign LORD, what can you give me since I remain childless and the one who will inherit my estate is Eliezer of Damascus?" And Abram said, "You have given me no children; so a servant in my household will be my heir." Then the word of the LORD came to him: "This man will not be your heir, but a son coming from your own body will be your heir".*

Genesis 15:2-5

Eliezer was the chief slave-servant of Abraham; the one in charge of everything in his household; the one who went to get a wife for Isaac. No matter how close and brotherly he was, 'something' in Abraham did not feel comfortable to leave the family inheritance to him. Abraham wanted his own son; born by him. The fullness of relationships is the spirit of Sonship. Son-ship has it all. A son-and-master relationship translates into a son-and-father relationship in the long run. A son goes all the way. He perceives no limitations except those of his own making. He can go all the way, to even as far as sacrificing his own life for the family venture. He would rather die than allow anything adverse to happen to the father's business. He believes, and firmly too, that after the father everything shall be passed to him. His thinking and actions are far superior to all the others already mentioned. He is much more interested in the father's business.

> *"Therefore come out from them and be separate, says the Lord. Touch no unclean thing, and I will receive you. I will be a Father to you, and you will be my sons and daughters, says the Lord Almighty".*

2 Corinthians 6:17-18

To live in the consciousness of sonship we must willingly decide to come out from the slave servant mentality, the friendly nature, and the selfish brotherly comfort to the level of son-ship, which is the level of selfless sacrifices, total commitment, faithfulness and obedience. There must be total and unshakable belief in the father and in his venture. It is written:

> *"But as many as received him, to them gave he power to become the sons of God, even to them that believe on his name: Which were born, not of blood, nor of the will of the flesh, nor of the will of man, but of God".*

John 1:12

There must be a paradigm shift in our ways of thinking, acting and behaving. We must totally destroy our former ways of thinking and renew our mind to that of a son.

> *Do not conform any longer to the pattern of this world,*
> *but be transformed by the renewing of your mind. Then*
> *you will be able to test and approve what God's will is-his*
> *good, pleasing and perfect will.*

> Romans 12:2

The pattern of this world is the slave-servant mentality; the pattern of this world is the friendly nature and the selfish brotherly comfort. The Israelites exhibited this when they left Egypt after four hundred years of slavery. They didn't want to leave the comfort zone they were used to. God had to take them through a process for forty years. Yet they found it hard and committed many atrocities because they wouldn't have a shift in mentality. At the end because they didn't shift mentally only a few of those that left Egypt actually entered the Promised Land even though they saw it. Their childen having had some influence from their fathers also had to be tested, Judges 3: 1-4. So, we see that all these are connected with the way we think, the way we talk and the way we do things. A friend of this world is limited from becoming a matured Son of God; and therefore becomes an enemy of God.

God's good and perfect will is for us to grow into maturity so that we can enjoy the fullness of Sonship. There are certain things babes cannot receive. Over the years these forms of thinking have held us bound from the enjoyment of the rights and privileges of a son. A slave-servant thinks and acts like a slave- servant; a friend thinks and acts like a friend; a brother thinks and acts like a brother; but a son thinks and acts like a son. To illustrate this, let me tell you of an incident that happened between a maid and her mistress.

A mistress had a very nice and wonderful maid and attempted to treat her as her only daughter. Whatever she bought herself she would buy for the maid. Wherever she went she would go with her. One day the king invited the mistress to a banquet in his palace in which they were required to spend a night. So she decided to go with her. For the king's banquet the mistress had to do a special shopping. Everything that was bought was in pairs: one for her and the other for her maid. They got beautifully dressed that the maid felt like the mistress and in her excitement walked up to the mistress and said to her politely "please as we go to the king's banquet do not call me a maid".

The mistress agreed and advised her not to think or act as a maid but to behave like a mistress. With this understanding they set out. Not too far from the palace they were drenched by sudden rain and as soon as they arrived at the palace the mistress went up to change into another dress, but the maid went by the fire side to dry her dress. She was there by the fire side when the mistress returned, and seeing her there, she exclaimed to the astonishment of the maid, "Maid go and change". Embarrassed but bold she responded and said, "Ma, I thought we agreed that you would not call me a maid?" To which the mistress retorted, "Yes, but we also agreed that you would not think or act like one".

We see that from this experience, no matter what the mistress did, the maid was still bound by her thinking, which governed her actions. Our thinking and our actions over the years have become part of us. It is not something we can suddenly change, even though they are within our control.

Consider this other scenario: Imagine that you are a slave-servant; friend or brother, and suddenly your very rich master, brother or friend says to you, "From today, you are my son." How would you respond and react?

Would you immediately accept and begin to think and act like a son? Certainly not! This is a very difficult thing to accept and to do. This is the case of people who are born again.

> *For he chose us in him before the creation of the world to be holy and blameless in his sight. In love he predestined us to be adopted as his sons through Jesus Christ, in accordance with his pleasure and will- to the praise of his glorious grace, which he has freely given us in the One he loves. In him we have redemption through his blood, the forgiveness of sins, in accordance with the riches of*

> *God's grace that he lavished on us with all wisdom and*
> *understanding.*

Ephesians 1:4-9

Changing our ways of thinking and acting can never be a sudden thing. It is a process. We cannot do it by ourselves. Hence the Bible says, "He gives us the power to be called the sons of God." God knows the difficulty of this task without Him and so He did not leave us alone to do it and that is why He gave us His Holy Spirit.

> *Therefore, brothers, we have an obligation-but it is not*
> *to the sinful nature, to live according to it. For if you live*
> *according to the sinful nature, you will die; but if by the*
> *Spirit you put to death the misdeeds of the body, you will*
> *live, because those who are led by the Spirit of God are*
> *sons of God. For you did not receive a spirit that makes*
> *you a slave again to fear, but you received the Spirit of*
> *son ship. And by him we cry, "Abba, Father." The Spirit*
> *himself testifies with our spirit that we are God's children.*
> *Now if we are children, then we are heirs-heirs of God and*
> *co-heirs with Christ, if indeed we share in his sufferings*
> *in order that we may also share in his glory.*

Galatians 4:6-7

# The Exalted Status Of A Son

*"For you did not receive a spirit that makes you a slave
again to fear, but you received the Spirit of sonship. And
by him we cry, 'Abba, Father. The Spirit himself testifies
with our spirit that we are God s children. Now if we are
children, then we are heirs".*

Romans 8:15-17a

It is not progressive and indeed painful for us to continue to live with
the slave- servant mentality; unsatisfactory for us to remain at the
friend realm, or to keep the brotherly mentality. Living at these levels
are self-limiting, and shut us out from enjoying the fullness of our divine
inheritance. These innate attitudes hinder us from growing into mature
Sons of God. God's desire is for all to be saved, become His adopted sons
and grow into maturity and fruitfulness to manifest His nature, power
and character. *Romans 1:2-4... regarding his son, who as to his human
nature was a descendant of David, and who through the Spirit of holiness
was declared with power to be the Son of God by his resurrection from
the dead.* This is 'the Secret Verse'. This is the heart cry of God and we
need to submit to His Holy Spirit if we must be transformed into the
likeness of His son.

*Therefore, since we have such a hope, we are very bold.
We are not like Moses, who would Put a veil over his face
to keep the Israelites from gazing at it while the radiance
was fading away. But their minds were made dull, for
to this day the same veil remains when the old covenant*

*is read. It has not been removed, because only in Christ is it taken away. Even to this day when Moses is read, a veil covers their hearts. But whenever anyone turns to the Lord, the veil is taken away. Now the Lord is the Spirit, and where the Spirit of the Lord is, there is freedom. And we, who with unveiled faces all reflect the Lord's glory, are being transformed into his likeness with ever-increasing glory, which comes from the Lord, who is the Spirit.*

2 Corinthians 3:12-18

Jesus Christ came to grant us the spirit of sonship, which is the ultimate essence of salvation. Sonship confers on us the full benefits of inheritance. The son is privy to all that the father does, is doing or will do. The son does nothing outside the father's directives. He submits his will totally to that of the father, and whatever the son asks of the father, he does. The son is the only one who can die for the father's business, because everything the father owns is his; actually made for him. No wonder no one else agreed to die for humanity. The others that came before Him were either slave-servants or friends or brothers. Jesus Christ is the begotten Son of God and through Him and in Him we have been adopted as sons of God. This is the reconciliation between man and God. God did not create slaves or servants or friends or brothers, but He made sons and daughters, and gave them an inheritance:

*And God said, Let us make man in our image, after our likeness: and let them have dominion over the fish of the sea, and over the fowl of the air, and over the cattle, and over all the earth, and over every creeping thing that creepeth upon the earth.*

*So God created man in his own image, in the image of God created he him; male and female created he them.*

*And God blessed them, and God said unto them, Be fruitful, and multiply, and replenish the earth, and subdue it: and have dominion over the fish of the sea, and over the fowl of the air, and over every living thing that moveth upon the earth.*

*And God said, Behold, I have given you every herb bearing seed, which is upon the face of all the earth, and every tree, in the which is the fruit of a tree yielding seed; to you it shall be for meat.*

*Genesis 1:26-29 (KJV)*

These powers are not for slave-servants or friends or brothers but for sons. Who would want to place all that he owns, and worked for in life in the hands of a slave-servant, friend or brother, and yet be happy? No one! Nobody can call this good, let alone very good. We lost the spirit of sonship in the Garden of Eden, but now we are offered the opportunity to regain it through Jesus Christ when we get saved and grow to maturity:

"*When I was a child, I talked like a child; I thought like a child, I reasoned like a child. When I became a man, I put childish ways behind me*".

1Corinthians 13:11

Also true is the kind of food we eat (Hebrews 5:11-14). As infants our principal food is milk. Milk has to do with elementary precepts of a believer. These are the basics. This is usually the road map to the ultimate, which is the manifestation of the spirit of sonship; without which we cannot enjoy the privileges and rights of a son. Building up our faith towards maturity has to do with our personal efforts and the grace of God: we must study to show ourselves approved; working out our own salvation; examining ourselves to see whether we are still in the faith or whether we are growing. Note that this is a typology of God's position in Judges 3:1-4. Since it has to do with us, no one can be used as an excuse for lack of growth. Think back to when we were newly born again; whatever we requested in prayers (and provided it was not detrimental to our life) God gave us quickly. As we grow, the time it takes for our prayer to be answered gets a bit more prolonged, as we are no longer infants, whose needs are easily and quickly taken care of. This is because God wants to teach us how to do things ourselves as He would do them. He wants to develop His nature and character in us so that we can represent Him effectively here on earth. The Bible is God's manual, which is one of the ways He uses to teach us what to do, by His Spirit. The experiences and knowledge gained is part of the evidence that equips us to teach others.

> *Praise be to the God and Father of our Lord Jesus Christ, the Father of compassion and the God of all comfort, who comforts us in all our troubles, so that we can comfort those in any trouble with the comfort we ourselves have received from God.*

2 Corinthians 1:3-4

As we begin to learn and do things, it becomes part of us and we become light of the world and salt of the earth, imparting others. As we continue to do so, we begin to be one with our Father God in nature and character, thus influencing people, policies, and governments, ushering in the new kingdom. This is the vision and wish of God.

> *Philip said, "Lord, show us the Father and that will be enough for us." Jesus answered: "Don't you know me, Philip, even after I have been among you such a long time? Anyone who has seen me has seen the Father. How can you say, 'Show us the Father'? Don t you believe that I am in the Father, and that the Father is in me? The words I say to you are not just my own. Rather, it is the Father, living in me, who is doing his work. Believe me when I say that lam in the Father and the Father is in me; or at least believe on the evidence of the miracles themselves.*

John 14: 8-11

Think back to when we were in school: lecturers lectured, teachers taught but afterwards we went back on our own to the library, sometimes taking additives to drive or keep off sleep, studying hard to make good grades. Think of professionals who after their academics are still subjected to practical exercises before finally qualifying to practice on their own. In the same vein, until we go in search of the knowledge that will make us grow into spiritual maturity we cannot enjoy the full benefit of the spirit of sonship. Maturity in sonship starts with us discovering the purpose of God. Everyone who has the spirit of the Son of God should overcome the world, but it is very difficult to overcome the world if we have not discovered our purpose. If we do not know where we are going it is difficult to find the right direction. Every direction becomes a way. It is imperative for us to be able to say to every of our situation, "It is written", as we go on acting our purpose.

> *It was he who gave some to be apostles, some to be prophets, some to be evangelists, and some to be pastors and teachers, to prepare God's people for works of service, so that the body of Christ may be built up until we all reach unity in the faith and in the knowledge of the Son of God and become mature, attaining to the whole measure of the fullness of Christ. Then we will no longer be infants, tossed back and forth by the waves, and blown here and there by every wind of teaching and by the cunning and craftiness of men in their deceitful scheming.*
>
> Ephesians 4:11-14

We need to come to the knowledge that through Jesus Christ we have been adopted as the sons of God, and behave likewise.

> *What I am saying is that as long as the heir is a child, he is no different from a slave, although he owns the whole estate. He is subject to guardians and trustees until the time set by his father. So also, when we were children, we were in slavery under the basic principles of the world. But when the time had fully come, God sent his Son, born of a woman, born under law, to redeem those under law, that we might receive the full rights of sons. Because you are sons, God sent the Spirit of his Son into our hearts, the*

*Spirit who calls out, "Abba, Father." So you are no longer a slave, but a son; and since you are a son, God has made you also an heir.*

Galatians 4:1-7

# *Attaining Maturity*

The heart desire of fathers is that their children grow into maturity and if possible surpass them. A father is always looking forward to the maturity of his children to fully empower them, handing down authority, power and all he has acquired. A father looks forward to this continuity with joy. Maturity brings us into the fullness of the manifestation of the character of sonship where we begin to enjoy all the rights and privileges that are due to us here on earth and full access to God in heaven, who tells us everything, hiding nothing from us. The son always has easy access to the father. It is also easier for people to get to fathers through their children, especially through the son of inheritance, who will take over the fathers business, than through a slave-servant, friend or brother:

> "I am the way and the truth and the life. No one comes
> to the Father except through me. If you really knew me,
> you would know my Father as well. From now on, you do
> know him and have seen him."
>
> John 14:6-7

The son's heartbeat now becomes that of the father. Whatever the son looks forward to, he just requests or commands and it will be granted, because the father's authority is with him. He takes charge completely. There is inner joy, satisfaction and security. We come into this sense of fulfillment knowing we are, and behaving like, a true son who's Father is God. This gives us confidence and we fear death no more. We have come into the full liberty of Adam before he sinned in the Garden of

Eden; we now become more than conquerors. This is the completion stage of growth, where peace, joy, and power begin to operate through us due to the anointing of the Holy Spirit; thus fulfilling the scripture that our body is the temple of the Holy Spirit. This growth in maturity, fruitfulness and manifestation as a son is 'The Secret Verse'.

Having become a fully mature son, identified in the body of Christ, exercising spiritual gifts, talents and abilities, we receive the inheritance of sonship. It then becomes incumbent to edify the body of Christ and expand the business by using our anointing to evangelize others to become sons and daughters and bring glory to God our Father.

Although sons and daughters have many privileges and rights, they should be very responsible and have good character as they are disciplined much more severely when they fail to carry out and obey instructions, fully. This is the father's love. It is the fathers' glory that no man should perish but should come to this knowledge of truth.

The Signs of Immaturity

> They hold firmly to their old unprogressive ways of thinking.
>
> They do not bear fruits.
>
> They do not know their purpose.
>
> They are mere churchgoers and so do nothing to build the church.
>
> Every form of doctrine tosses them up and down.
>
> They look more unto men rather than unto God.
>
> They dwell much more on the elementary principles.
>
> They cannot take initiatives so you must remind them of everything again and again.
>
> They are not really planted in any church so they jump from church to church looking for where they can be spoon-fed; giving the reason that they are looking for God.

They allow men to hinder their spiritual growth, using them as excuses.

They are slaves to law.

They do not give freely to the work of God.

They are cajoled to work for God.

They give excuses for nearly everything they are asked to do.

They quarrel and argue over elementary issues, forgetting weightier matters.

They look outwards rather than inwards.

They are corrected on issues again and again.

They want to, protect, defend and fight for God

They are full of excuses of "why and but".

They hate being corrected, rebuked or disciplined.

They are still servants or slaves; because they are not of age to operate their fathers' will. They remain under custodians because they are still minors and do not know much about the father's business. They do not or cannot know the principles of the kingdom.

The list is inexhaustive; just imagine all the traits and characteristics of babies, they are the very traits and characteristics of immature Christians

# Making Your Sonship Sure

Accepting adoption (from God) is not easy, and remaining an adopted son or daughter is even harder. Sometimes even biological children get so frustrated in the process of training that they deny their parents as parents. If biological children do this much, imagine how an adopted child would feel when the adoptive father is taking him through the process of maturing into sonship. God knew that this would not be an easy process that is why He gave us His Holy Spirit. Even with His Spirit we need to make a choice to accept to be adopted as a son or daughter to the end. It must be tested. His Spirit will not force us to accept His good intentions of adoption. 'Something' in us, our inner mind would want to persecute, rebel and make us feel unworthy, or cause us to believe that we are reaping where we did not sow: Or we may doubt that our adoption and acceptance as a son or daughter is real; that a day would come we may be denied or cast away. Our Father is faithful. He will never forsake us, even when we pass through difficulties or fail He remains faithful to us; He is not a man that He will lie.

God's Spirit in us shows us how, and what to do to sustain sonship. We are to make our sonship sure by submitting to the direction of the Spirit of God. This requires total obedience and willingness. Submitting to God comes by godly faith. Godly faith sustains the spirit of sonship, otherwise pressures from people's opinion and the world will hinder us, to make us lose the place of sonship. It is important to note that nothing can happen outside faith. Every man has a measure of faith and without faith we cannot exist. The only difference is what the faith can make us believe and do.

*By faith Moses, when he had grown up, refused to be known as the son of Pharaoh's daughter. He chose to be mistreated along with the people of God rather than to enjoy the pleasures of sin for a short time. He regarded disgrace for the sake of Christ as of greater value than the treasures of Egypt, because he was looking ahead to his reward.*

Hebrews 11:24-27

Moses, by godly faith, refused to be adopted as a son by the daughter of one of the richest kings in his day, despising the privilege to enjoy the pleasures of Egypt. This goes to explain that acceptance to be adopted, as a son is a choice that goes beyond mere pleasures and comforts of life. Pleasures and comforts are temporary. Short-term thoughts come from worldly faith, which are usually the attributes of servants. Sons look at eternal values; values that can be passed from generation to generation without fear. The kind of faith that sustains us as son is the faith that looks ahead to the reward from God rather than the pleasures of men and the world. This kind of faith endures hardship; it knows and believes that the end will be better than the beginning; the kind of faith that says in every situation "it shall work out for my good because my father God is in control". True faith looks at things seen as temporal while things unseen are eternal. God, in His love has given us ability and power to participate in His divine nature. Through this nature we can escape the corruption in the world caused by evil desires; the desires that will make us compromise our son-ship for short-term pleasures.

*For this very reason, make every effort to add to your faith goodness; and to goodness, knowledge; and to knowledge, self-control; and to self-control, perseverance; and to perseverance, godliness; and to godliness, brotherly kindness; and to brotherly kindness, love. For if you possess these qualities in increasing measure, they will keep you from being ineffective and unproductive in your knowledge of our Lord Jesus Christ. But if anyone does not have them, he is nearsighted and blind, and has forgotten that he has been cleansed from his past sins.*

2 Peter 1:5-9

To make sonship effective, productive and sure we need to grow beyond the faith that brought us into the adoption of sonship. We need to add to our faith goodness, knowledge, self-control, perseverance, brotherly kindness and love. These qualities will greatly enhance our knowledge, which will in turn affect our actions as a son or daughter. Mature sons and daughters are those who know, understand and do the principles of the Kingdom. They have the blueprint. Mature sonship empowers us to know what doors to open; what doors to shut: who to allow into our house and who not to. Mature Sons and daughters are charismatic; characterized by dignity and humility; gentle, loveable and can easily be identified among the crowd. These qualities are within our control but will require personal training and development. By them we sustain the spirit of sonship, which will lead to everlasting wealth, keep us focused till we receive a rich welcome into the eternal kingdom of our Father God, in heaven. Never forget that word of encouragement that addresses us as a son, for in it we have strength and hope to carry on in times of great difficulties, challenges and oppositions. Remember God is always glad to treat us as a son, and always watching to see how we expand His business and treat His other children, especially those He has appointed to lead

# Points To Note

Faith is the foundation of sonship: the pathway to "The Secret Verse". Belief is the doing of faith that leads to the adoption into Sonship. Belief grows by what we hear from others (John 4:39) through to deeper self-conviction by studies and Godly encounter (John 4:42), until made practical and doable, with results for others to see. Maturity and fruitfulness is the ultimate goal of believes, leading to sonship.

Sonship makes relationship with God very easy "...My yoke is easy and my burden is light". Sons do not accept the testimonies or praises of men (John 5:34 & 41) concerning them, but only that which comes from God whom they are accountable to. Sons, whether in the physical or spiritual must grow to maturity to enjoy the fullness of a will. Mature sons are conscious of God in all that they think, say or do. It is about Godly character.

Mature sons do nothing by themselves but only what they see the Father do, because whatever the Father does the son also does, for the Father loves the son and shows him all that he does. (John 5:19-20).

*Nevertheless, God's solid foundation stands firm, sealed with this inscription: "The Lord knows those who are his," and, "Everyone who confesses the name of the Lord must turn away from wickedness." 11Tim 2:19.* Therefore live by the Spirit, and you will not gratify the desires of the sinful nature... Gal 5:16-18

If you genuinely said the sinners prayers in chapter 7 please e-mail the author for further assistance.

God bless you

When I was a child, I spake as a child, I understood as a child, I thought as a child: but when I became a man, I put away childish things.

1Cor 13:11(KJV)

I will declare the decree: the LORD hath said unto me, Thou art my Son; this day have I begotten thee.

Ask of me, and I shall give thee the heathen for thine inheritance, and the uttermost parts of the earth for thy possession.

Thou shalt break them with a rod of iron; thou shalt dash them in pieces like a potter's vessel.

Psalm 2:7-9 (KJV)

So I say, walk by the Spirit, and you will not gratify the desires of the flesh. For the flesh desires what is contrary to the Spirit. They are in conflict with each other, so that you are not to do whatever you want. But if the Spirit leads you, you are not under the law... the acts of the flesh are ...

Galatians 5:16-26

"As believers we have the seed of God in us, but we need to be determined to make effort to become the sons and daughters of God, in nature and character in order to dominate and reign forever".

Author

... a door has been opened, enter and be adopted ...